# Capture Your Own Style with Collage Quilting

## Making Unique Quilts and Projects from Photos and Imagery

Jane Haworth

# Dedication

To my parents, Michael and Sally, for encouraging my art and craft endeavors growing up.

*Capture Your Own Life with Collage Quilting*

Landauer Publishing, www.landauerpub.com, is an imprint of Fox Chapel Publishing Company, Inc.

Copyright © 2023 by Jane Haworth and Fox Chapel Publishing Company, Inc.,
903 Square Street, Mount Joy, PA 17552.

Project Team
Managing Editor: Gretchen Bacon
Acquisitions Editor: Amelia Johanson
Editor: Christa Oestreich
Designer: Mary Ann Kahn
Proofreader & Indexer: Jean Bissell

Contributor photos and captions are courtesy of their associated artist (unless otherwise stated), used with permission
Step-by-step photos and all other photography (unless otherwise stated) by Jane Haworth
Studio photography by Mike Mihalo: back cover (all); pages 4–5 (all), 57 (top), 64–65, 67, 73, 78, 79, 85, 91, 97, 101, 104, 105, 111, 114, 115, 119, 124, 125.
Photography by Amelia Johanson: pages 58 (bottom), 59–60 (all).
Shutterstock used for backgrounds: Alina Kholopova (front cover, 1), Followtheflow (67), Alena Ozerova (73), Eastmanka (79), Kite_rin (85), robert_s (91), brizmaker (97), Pixel-Shot (101), Peyker (105), Rawpixel.com (111), Art Stocker (115), Yuri-U (119), united photo studio (125).

ISBN 978-1-63981-022-2

Library of Congress Control Number: 2023939042

We are always looking for talented authors. To submit an idea, please send a brief inquiry to acquisitions@foxchapelpublishing.com.

Note to Professional Copy Services:
The publisher grants you permission to make up to six copies of any quilt patterns in this book for any customer who purchased this book and states the copies are for personal use.

Printed in China
First printing

# Acknowledgments

To my husband, Martin, who puts food on our table, cooks it all too, and ignores all the quilting supplies that are taking over the house! To my daughters, Lucy and Becky, who have been my invaluable editors throughout my writing journey. Thank you for the encouragement! And to my son, James, who is always happy to loan me his camera and be on hand to take photographs for me!

Without the encouragement and support of my local quilt guild Foothill Quilters Guild in Auburn, California, I would not have followed this path in quilting. I joined this group in 2005 as a novice quilter. I sewed all my life growing up in the UK, but the quilting scene was totally foreign to me. My first speaking engagements were to these ladies, and I was incredibly nervous. They are still my best quilting friends. Through their encouragement, and with opportunities to meet amateur and professional quilters at work, my quilting career blossomed.

To the Mountain Art Quilters of Nevada City who, from the beginning, were an aspirational group that I dreamed of joining. Now, as part of this talented group of ladies, they put up with me when I am too busy to attend meetings or when I am traveling to teach. I also want to thank my friend Sandra Bruce for supplying the handmade polymer clay button that I used on the Seashell Purse. I love your earrings too, Sandra. And to Pokey Bolton who took a chance on me and published my first article in *Quilting Arts* magazine in 2011. Her encouragement took me from being a student at her Craft Napa retreats to being a teacher.

Thanks to all my students who enjoy my technique and run with it! They are enthusiastic and encourage me to get up every day to come up with new ideas and patterns.

I would also like to thank these companies for donating some of the supplies I used when making the projects for this book:

- Moda Fabrics for supplying the beautiful fabric for the Maxi Dog Quilt without which this quilt would have been truly scrappy.

- Thanks to WonderFil® Specialty Threads for their generosity, and to Samantha for educating me about threads, as normally I would have chosen thread only by color!

- Tina Hilton at Turtle Hand Batik who was so generous with her donation of fabrics for the Colorful Cat Pillow. She spent a long time seeking out her small pieces of fabric, which were perfect for me.

- Thank you to Karen Kay Buckley for the 6" (15.2cm) scissors. KKB makes the best scissors for fabric collage, and you can never have too many pairs!

- Also, to Terry McFeely of Terial Magic who donated her wonderful stiffening spray for me to use on the fabric for my projects.

Finally, thanks to Amelia Johanson at Landauer Publishing for finding my work online and encouraging me to submit a proposal. Although I had considered writing a book for a long time, I finally made time to focus on this endeavor.

—Jane H

# Contents

96

66

78

84

114

110

72

104

90

100

# Introduction

I love making colorful art quilts inspired by nature, my travels, and my home. I like to think my style is representational, although serendipitous and a little quirky! Many of my designs start with a photo as inspiration. In this book, I will guide you through my approach to collage quilting and techniques to help you successfully complete collage projects. My wish is to encourage everyone to stop looking for perfection, have fun with the creative process, and not fear tackling new projects. I believe my fabric collage technique is doable for all levels of quilters and artists, from novices to more experienced sewists. I do not want you to think that this is beyond your skills or expertise. We all have *creativity* within us.

I have been sewing and crafting as long as I can remember. At eleven years old, I entered a granny square crocheted vest, which I designed myself, into the local Christmas Fair. My cousin Amanda and I would spend our summers learning new crafts from puppet design to soap making. I was never afraid to design my own sweater, dress, curtains, or soap! This is the approach I take in all my creative endeavors. When introduced to quilting, I experimented with using patterns, but the freedom of creating my own designs from my photos and memories kept me interested. Now, 20 years later, the course of my collage journey continues to grow and develop as my inspiration source never runs dry!

I don't think of myself as a natural artist. I am not able to pick up a pencil and draw something

**Create something "sweet" for yourself or as a gift for a friend or family member.**

amazing, but I notice that the more I practice, the smoother my skills become and what I produce is better. In this book, I am not expecting you to be an artist, rather just to have the courage to start the artistic process! The more you repeat or practice a process, the easier it will become, you'll be more relaxed, and the results will be sweet!

Colorful quilts of all kinds can be made with fabric collage. Capture your favorite animals, flowers, or treasured memories in a beautiful display!

# Collage Quilting

Fabric collage is a simple, fun, and slightly addictive process. The combination of a personalized design, fabric choices, and the love you put into the project will lead you to completing a unique and successful quilt. My approach to collage is spontaneous, serendipitous, and freeing with few rules or parameters. For these projects, we are not going for photorealism as we trace, cut, and layer. I do not spend time making pattern pieces first. I work directly over the pattern, tracing and cutting my shapes and making immediate progress. The collage will start to take shape quickly.

Most of the themes in this book are inspired by nature, animals, birds, fish, flowers, and more. You might notice I have not included any designs for people and faces made in collage. These are another great source for inspiration, but I felt this theme could be a whole book in itself. You

## The Definition of Collage

Collage, from the French verb *coller*, meaning "to glue," is the artistic process of gluing and assembling various materials to a flat surface. Collage can refer to both the actual procedure of cutting and pasting (the verb), as well as to the final artistic product (the noun).

RAW-EDGE FABRIC COLLAGE is collage made by cutting fabric and keeping the raw edges, not turning or hiding the fabric edge as in appliqué.

My technique makes it easy to recreate photographs, which is great for immortalizing your beloved pets.

can certainly use my techniques and apply them to making a collage from a photo of a friend or relative. In the gallery, you will see one face quilt I have made.

Fabric collage starts with a line drawing. I am most comfortable starting with a photo when looking for my design or quilt inspiration. Using a photo, I trace the lines to produce my line drawing or pattern. This can be enlarged to any size needed. In this book, I will guide you through this process and make you comfortable and less fearful about making your own pattern. You will be your own quilt designer!

I have traveled all over the US and internationally teaching collage classes. Whether it's Dubai or Houston, Texas, one of my most popular classes is Love of Pets, or Pet Portraits. Students enjoy working on making a quilt of their own pet or favorite animal rather than working on a generic dog or cat pattern. The time and love invested in a project like this is always present. Often students will make a quilt as a gift for someone who has lost their pet as a way of passing on their love. On page 40, Guide to Making Animals and Pets will offer more tips when creating these types of quilts.

I've had the pleasure of teaching fabric collage to students around the world. I hope you are encouraged to try these projects and enjoy the freedom in this approach.

Once you master fabric collage, you'll be making larger and more intricate pieces in no time.

Over the years, I have taught many children to work on sewing arts projects, and I have heard many of them treasure the items that they made. As adults, we need to embrace fearlessness in the same way children approach art and sewing. Some of my best free-motion quilting students have been children, as they don't have those nagging doubts about things not being good enough or looking as they are "supposed to look." They just go for it! Your first collage quilts may not be perfect. Don't dwell on the imperfections—relish the experience. Then make another collage, as you will have learned something during that process.

## What to Expect

This book is divided into a technique section and a project section. The project quilts are made in different sizes and uses. I have various wall hangings, a tote bag, a pillow, table runner, and even a bed-size quilt. When you are making your collage, I am giving you permission to use the project designs and patterns for whatever purpose or size you wish. I describe how I used the design and what size I enlarged it to, but there are no rules that say you must do the same. For example, Heart and Home measures about 14" x 20" (35.6 x 50.8cm), but it could be fun to see this as a larger wall hanging. I made Colorful Cat into a 20" (50.8cm) pillow, but you could change things up and use the pattern to make a wall hanging or tote bag.

For some of the projects in this book, I have provided a pattern so you can make your own version of the project. See Patterns on page 142. In other projects, I encourage you to take on the challenge of designing and making your own pattern and personal quilt. In Heart and Home, I have used a photo of my house to make the quilt. My instructions are written so you can create a personalized version of your own home or the house of a friend or family member.

My desire is for this book to be your instruction manual for making unique and personal quilts. But it can also be the tool that guides you and builds your confidence in creative freedom to create special projects. Let's get collaging!

# chapter 1

# Getting Started

## Supplies

There are many methods to create fabric collage. For example, I use glue in my collage and not fusible products as others do. I get asked "Is the glue hard to stitch through?" No. I am using minimal glue; it just secures the pieces until they are sewn down. The resulting quilt is easy to stitch through and it remains soft and subtle without fusible layers inside. I want readers to feel happy when making these quilts, so I give you permission to use a different method if that makes it easier for you.

What I appreciate about fabric collage is that it does not require a huge inventory of supplies. Once you find your favorite tools, you will probably just stick with those. Not including fabric, the supplies are small, lightweight, and easy to tote around so you can collage with friends or at events.

## Basic Tools

This is an exhaustive list of tools that you will need, including some of my favorite products. Once you figure out your preferred tools, you will not need all those listed below. Instead, you'll create a tool kit that will cover most of your work.

- **Black permanent markers**. I use Sharpie Ultra Fine and Fine Point. The thick dark line is good to use when drawing on a black-and-white enlarged photo. When tracing over a 8" x 10" (20.3 x 25.4cm) photo onto regular or tracing paper, the ultra-fine pen is good for drawing finer details that will later be enlarged.

- **Regular ink pen**. In a pinch, I will use a regular pen when tracing shapes for collage. This is only when my pencil or chalk-marker lines are not showing up on a particular fabric. Remember to cut on this line.

- **Chalk marker** or **pencil**. Choose a suitable fabric marker depending on the fabric color. I use a chalk marker on dark fabric and a pencil on light fabric. The chalk marker I like to use the most is the BOHIN Mechanical Chalk Pencil or the Chaco Liner, both of which can be refilled.

- **Disappearing ink pen** (optional). Pilot FriXion erasable pens claim ink marks drawn on fabric will disappear with heat, so you just need to iron them away. I would use this kind of pen in the same way as the regular ink pen.

- **Fabric scissors**. I use regular or larger fabric scissors when cutting my fabric down so it is a smaller and more usable size to work with.

- **Small sharp scissors**. These are used specifically for collage. I use Karen Kay Buckley 6" (15.2cm) Perfect Scissors. This type of scissor has a fine serrated edge that grips the fabric as it is cut. This is great for cutting small pieces in collage. Highly recommended and a game changer!

- **Rotary cutter** and **cutting mat**. In collage, I don't regularly use these basic quilts tools: cutting mat, rotary cutter, and ruler. But when it comes to cutting borders, binding fabrics, or squaring up your quilt, these tools are essential.

- **Fabric glue** and a **glue applicator**. Something like a coffee stirrer would be a cheap option. There are various glues that work in collage, so try what you have and are most comfortable using. I like to put Aleene's Original Tacky Glue in a small container and use the flat glue spreader to apply. A needle-nosed glue bottle works also. Using these tools means you don't need to move the pieces to apply the glue.

- **Tweezers.** Heidi Proffetty has some great ones.

- **Painter's tape or masking tape.** Useful for many jobs as it has a temporary hold and is easily removed. Tape will hold paper to the window when using that method for tracing. When tracing over a photo, I will tape my two layers together so things don't shift. It's also important to tape the foundation to the pattern when you start to collage. The most useful size I like to use is 1"–1½" (2.5–3.8cm) wide.

- **Pins.** I don't use a lot of pins in my sewing. I think this is because I was trained on a production line in a factory where pins are not used! I do use them to temporarily hold my collage in place when stitching a background. Or when stitching seams on a bag or similar item. Quilters pins or Magic Pins are long and have a nice, large grip or head.

- **Quilt rulers.** For me, the most useful ruler is the 6" x 24" (15.2 x 61cm). I use it for cutting strips for a binding, trimming the sides of a quilt, and measuring. The square 12½" (31.8cm) ruler is used when squaring up the corners of a quilt.

- **Light box** or **light pad** (optional). You can buy light pads designed for quilters that may include various accessories or purchase a basic one for art that is less expensive. You may need this to make the pattern, but taping it to a window works perfectly. Some people like to use a light box while making the collage.

## PAINT SUPPLIES

These are my basic painting supplies that I use when painting a watercolor-type background. I encourage students to use what they already own and not to spend a lot of money on these. Inexpensive acrylic paints that can be purchased at a big-box craft store work; a plastic plate for mixing and foam brushes or inexpensive paint brushes do the job also. The painted fabric I use in my quilts is not meant as a focal point but to blend into and soften a plain background.

- **Liquid fabric stabilizer spray.** I prefer using Terial Magic. This is a nice product that stiffens the fabric, making it cut like paper. When cutting very small pieces it is a great help. It also prevents the fraying of the fabric, and it washes out when you're all done.

- **Test fabric.** Use a scrap of fabric from the final piece you'll be painting. This way you can test colors before starting, which can save a lot of heartache!

- **Acrylic or fabric paints.** The main difference is how they bond to the fabric. Since you are less likely to wash these projects, it's okay to use acrylic paint. If you want something more permanent, then use fabric paint, or mix your acrylic with fabric paint.

- **Paintbrush.** To get the watercolor effect that I use in these collage pieces, a large paintbrush or foam brush will do the trick. Small paintbrushes are used for detail.

- **Water container.** Use anything you have on hand!

- **Palette.** You can also use a plate for mixing colors.

- **Plastic table covering.** Protect your table or work surface from mess. This can be as simple as a place mat for small projects or a cheap plastic tablecloth for large pieces.

## Collage Supplies

- Scissors
- Chalk marker
- Pencil
- Glue and applicator
- Painter's tape

These are my go-to tools that are very easy to carry around. I've been known to work on fabric collage projects in hotels while teaching and traveling.

A colorful quilt usually means more thread colors because you want the thread to blend in with the main image rather than distract from it.

## THREADS

Because I collage using glue, thread is only needed near the end of the process. For many projects, this will be when free-motion quilting (page 52). However, I also recommend using some thread to accent an animal portrait, which can be for whiskers, fur, or other textural elements.

I have a large and varied collection of threads and select what to use based on the color fabric I am stitching over. The thread thickness I use is 40 or 50wt. I have been enjoying using WonderFil Specialty Threads; 50wt plain color is called Konfetti™ and 50wt variegated is called Tutti™. Using variegated colored thread is a great way to bring a random, dynamic variety of colors into your stitching without having to physically change the thread. For my projects, I typically use between 4 and 10 different thread colors, changing them out numerous times.

For the bobbin thread, I use Superior Threads' Bottom Line, which is a polyester 60wt and is finer. I choose a color that blends with my backing fabric, and I'm ready to go. Using this single bobbin thread means that I am not changing out the bobbin every time I change my top thread.

## Sewing Machine and Supplies

- Sewing machine, set up for free motion quilting
- Scissors
- Selection of colored threads and bobbin thread
- Gloves
- Pins

# Pattern Supplies

It doesn't take much to create a pattern, just a picture, paper, drawing tools, tape, and a light box.

Interfacing makes the perfect foundation to building your collage on because it's sturdy enough to hold your fabric but thin enough to sew through.

Most fabric collage will start with a black line drawing. Think of a coloring book page. Instead of using paints or crayons, you are cutting out fabric shapes to fill in sections. These supplies will help you to make a pattern of your image or photo.

- A **photo** of your theme. Make it 8" x 10" (20.3 x 25.4cm), printed in color or black & white.

- **Copy paper** or **vellum**, size 9" x 11" (22.9 x 28cm). Both are great to use as tracing paper. Parchment paper or vellum can be used to protect your pattern from glue as you collage while still seeing the lines underneath.

- **Freezer paper** has become an invaluable quilt tool and is found at the grocery store! One side is dull, the other shiny. You are able to draw onto the dull side and iron the shiny side onto your fabric for a temporary hold. I use this when making my lettering or small details. For example: Draw your word onto the dull side and cut it out, leaving about a ½" (1.3cm) allowance. Iron onto your fabric. Using your small collage scissors, cut precisely on the drawn lines. Fine details can be cut out this way, especially if you treat the fabric first with a stiffener.

- **Interfacing** or **stabilizer**. The interfacing acts as a foundation that the fabric pieces will eventually be attached to, and it keeps your finished collage as one unit. It does not need to be fusible. I use either Pellon® 810 Tru-Grid™ or Pellon 830 Easy Pattern®. Both of these are lightweight, and you can see the black lines of the pattern through them.

- **Copier, scanner,** and **printer**. I use my copier to scan the patterns and then print them out as PDFs. If you don't have these at home, you can take files on a memory stick to your local print shop. They should be able to help you with printing enlargements or photos.

- **Pencil**. A No. 2 pencil will do, since this is just to trace your image on paper. You can also use a mechanical pencil if you prefer.

- **Black permanent markers**. See page 11 for more information.

Fabric collage is the perfect use for your scraps! It's amazing how even the most unusual print can be repurposed.

# Fabrics

Textiles and fabric have played a big part in my life. I think almost every job I have had included fabrics as part of it. I am sure I am no different than many of you, but fabrics and textiles make me happy. Maybe it is the abundance of color and pattern that adds richness to my life or the memories that come with handling textiles.

For collage, all kinds of fabrics work. They can include old clothes that have been saved, fabrics that have been given to you, ones you have purchased, vintage linens, silks, and sheers. Supporting your local quilt store is important, so given the opportunity to shop for something specific, I will do that too. Successful collage requires a wide variety of small pieces, so it works out great in using up your scraps. Storing and sorting those scraps can be more of an issue though! Upcycling and reusing textiles in our collage quilting is a good practice, as textile waste is a huge worldwide issue. In the section Choosing a Background, I will talk more about other types of fabrics that can be used here.

These are the fabrics you want to have on hand for the projects in this book:

- A **variety of fabrics**, including light, medium, and dark values. If you are going for a realistic look

## Batting

For my collage quilts, I use a 100% cotton batting. It is thin, has good drape, and is easy to work with. There are many kinds of batting to choose from, including wool, 80/20 cotton/polyester, and bamboo. Use your favorite or whatever you have available.

(i.e., trying to match what you see in the photo) match the colors you see.

- Small amounts of **black and white fabric**.

- **Printable fabric sheets**. If you want to create your own fabric print, it's very easy to insert these sheets into your printer and have a unique piece in seconds. These can be photos, scans of memorabilia, or found illustrations that are free to use. I prefer using Jacquard Cotton Inkjet Fabric Sheets.

- **Background fabric, batting, backing fabric, and threads** for stitching. These will be needed to finish your quilt or quilting project.

## Selecting Your Fabrics

When selecting fabric for collage, I usually buy a fat quarter or smaller. If I see fabrics that would be a perfect background, I purchase 1 yard (91cm). Most of the time, you are only using small pieces from 1″–4″ (2.5–10cm), so I find I throw very little away and have many tubs of scraps.

Collecting fabrics in all values is also important. What I mean is light, medium, and dark shades of each color. My red collection can range from burgundy to claret, and rust to pink. I like to encourage students to *exaggerate* the colors they see to include all the values. Diversity in your fabric collection is also important as different types of fabric, prints, and patterns add spice and interest to your collage.

## Different Kinds of Fabrics

Here, learn about the kind of fabrics I like to use in my collage. My best suggestion is to use what you have to get started. Then in Choosing a Background, I will talk more about the types of fabric I use to complete the quilt.

**Batiks.** These fabrics are a good choice. Their tight weave means they don't fray as much which can help when working with raw edges. There is a richness in the depth and subtle variety in the color in plain batiks. Use tone on tone, printed batiks for small prints, or the lovely natural hand-dyed look of the jewel or lava batiks.

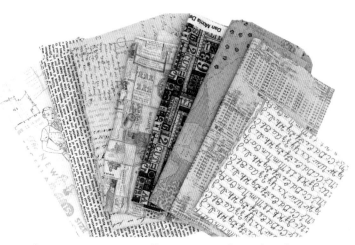

**Graphic type prints.** Small patterns and graphic designs work in collage. I am drawn to text, writing designs, and collaged prints. Using these unexpected designs in your collage will add interest.

## Taking Photos

**I chose a selection of red fabrics (left) and tried arranging from dark to light. A black and white view (right) reveals their values.**

Sometimes, colors and prints can make it hard to tell what value the overall fabric has. Take photos of your fabric selections arranged in order, then alter that photo with a filter to black and white. This will allow you to see the true value range of the fabrics chosen.

Also, using your phone to take photos while you work on your collage will give your eyes and brain a different perspective. I often say, "It looks better in the photo than in real life!"

## Tip

The more fabric options you have to work with, the easier it is for fabric collage. You won't get stuck wondering what fabric to use next or having to repeat one fabric continually. Hopefully raiding your scraps can provide all the fabrics you need in a small project.

**Texture prints.** This selection of fabric is all about the print. Many remind me of fur or animal skins. They can be used in landscapes for trees, grass, or skies. Using the design in the print and cutting it in the right orientation or direction can be perfect.

**Plain or solids.** Combined with print fabrics, I include a few plain fabrics. Many of my plain fabrics are not a flat solid but one color with some variation, like Moda Grunge fabrics. Hand-dyed fabrics are good for that subtle variation. Ombres have a gentle change in value and can add a lot of variety in one fabric. They are good for backgrounds as well.

**Black and white fabrics.** When making animal quilts, students are concerned what to do when their animal is a single color like black or white. If you collect enough variety of these fabrics, you will see the subtle variation in the values.

**Tip**

Don't forget to also look at the back of the fabric, as you paid for that too!

**Large or small prints.** I tend to use a lot of small prints or textures, but I am not afraid to include some larger prints. If you look carefully at large prints and specific details, these are good for fussy cutting. Use the fabric design or change of value in the print to create dimension in your collage. Let the fabric do the work for you.

**Unusual fabrics.** I usually use quilter's cottons, but all kinds of textiles can work. I have been known to include upholstery fabrics, burlaps, silks, sheers, clothing, bedding, and table linens. By using raw-edge fabrics, with no fusible on the back, things will fray. I accept this and it doesn't stop me. Rough texture and fraying can be what you are going for, especially in a landscape type of quilt. I also save selvages and look for specific words or phrases that I can include as part of my theme.

# Design, Color, and Composition

When starting out on a new project, I select a photo or image that excites me. Sometimes I know in advance what the project will be used for and have an idea of the size and color. Other times, I don't yet have a plan and am just excited to see where the creative process will take me.

Most of my collage work is made using a single image. I create my collage from an enlarged pattern by choosing, cutting, and gluing my fabrics in place. I spend much of my time and focus on the construction of the detailed image. Once it is completed, I choose a suitable background fabric to place it onto.

My design thought process:

**1.** Will this quilt be a gift, wall hanging, pillow, bag, or part of a jacket? Or will I challenge myself to make a big quilt for a quilt show?

**2.** What enlargement size to the photo do I need for this project?

**3.** Am I going to make the image look as it does in the photo, or could I choose an unconventional color scheme?

**4.** Do I have other related elements to include as part of the theme or design?

**5.** Do I have all the supplies and fabric I will need?

I hope learning about color and composition will help you when thinking about designing your own quilt or project. Sometimes design and color choices will happen intuitively depending on your project, or you may need to spend more time considering what to make. When I find a photo I love, or am up for a new challenge, I look through my new fabrics and make a quilt to include these. Or I might go to my scrap boxes, gather fabrics from a particular color family, and focus on those for my quilt. Currently, I am making chickens in the colors of the rainbow; I'm not sure where this will lead, but it is fun!

## Collage Size

Much of my work starts with a photo to base my pattern on. Before deciding on the size you need, there are a few things to consider:

- **Small size.** A collage made using a detailed 8" x 10" (20.3 x 25.4cm) photo can be tricky as the details will be very small to work with. It can be a challenge to cut them out in fabric, and because we're working with raw-edge fabric, the small pieces might fray.

- **Large size.** When making a very large collage, you might want to divide your pattern into sections that can be created individually and then sewn together at the end of the process. This will make things easier to handle.

Collages can be made small and detailed. It's more effort, but the results are worth it.

When making this large giraffe collage, I made the tongue, head, and neck as separate units. They came together when I attached them to the background.

Fabric collages can get very large very quick. Knowing how much space you have available is a good way to determine your theme and size, such as this relatively small chicken.

- **Use or purpose.** Knowing how the collage will be used will dictate the approximate size you will need. If you are creating a fixed-size pillow cover or mounting your collage on an art canvas, you will know the finished size you require. With a wall hanging or gift, you have more flexibility for the finished size.

- **Workspace.** When choosing a project size, I always take into consideration the workspace that I have available. I prefer to make collage on a horizontal tabletop since my technique involves drawing on the fabric by tracing the pattern, which is hard to do if it's hung vertically on a design wall.

## SCALE

I use scale either in the size of the image used or the size of the quilt made. Consider a photo of flowers: A quilt could be made showing all the flowers, or you could crop a portion of the image showing a single flower, enlarge it, and use that detail. These two designs could be made either as a large quilt or as a smaller wall hanging, and they would both look totally different.

In this photo, the geometric nature of this succulent was what stood out to me most. I thought it would be interesting to enhance that element even more by zooming in and focusing on only a selection of the plant. The results can be stunning!

# Composition

When designing a quilt, it's always good to consider the placement of the image. Should it be centered, off centered, attached to the bottom of the quilt, or floating? The asymmetrical placement of your design will create more energy and interest than simply being placed in the center. Placement usually depends on the image itself, and you can try different placements to see what looks best.

## Rule of Thirds

The rule of thirds is a compositional guide that places an image or images within an imaginary grid of three columns by three rows. The asymmetrical placement of design elements creates a pleasing composition. It is where the eye's gaze would naturally fall.

This dog is aligned almost perfectly on the right and bottom lines. Where they cross is next to the eye, which draws the eye to that focal point.

### ATTACHED OR FLOATING FOCAL IMAGES

When working with a focal image, like an animal portrait, I will remove any unnecessary elements (including some of the body) to keep the focus on the head. This provides a choice of placing the portrait either at the bottom of the quilt or centering it in the middle of the quilt. If the design is placed at the bottom of the quilt, I call it "attached" as it starts on an outer border of the quilt. If the portrait is centered in the quilt, it is "floating." I will finish the neckline of the focal image in a softened, uneven fashion of cut fabrics, then surround the image with the background fabric.

This dog quilt is "attached." The main image continues until the edge of the blanket.

This cow quilt is "floating." There is space between the bottom edge and where the cow cuts off.

When making a quilt design of multiple elements, such as chickens or vases, I include a horizontal line detail in the background so the components are grounded in some way; therefore, they are not "floating" in the composition. This horizontal line could be something like grass or a pathway for the chickens, or a tabletop for the vase. These choices are yours to make but should be considered in your design process.

The chickens look grounded in the piece because they are standing on the dirt. This option is handy if you don't want your focal image to "float."

## REPETITION IN DESIGN

If you wish to create unity in a design, repeating an image or theme will bring a cohesiveness and sense of pattern. Repeating an item three times, or with an odd-numbered grouping, looks more natural and appealing to the eye.

## COMPOSITION QUILTS

I like to call a quilt with a theme, narrative, or story a composition quilt. These quilts are usually a combination of different units made in a variety of mediums. When designing a composition quilt, I have a rough idea for the overall quilt arrangement, but it will not be finalized until I have all the elements gathered. By using a design wall, I cohesively bring all the elements together into the quilt design.

Travel journal quilts are what I call quilts that are inspired by a trip or vacation. The Travel Journal Quilt (page 118) tells a story. I included collaged flowers, photos, and postcards printed onto fabric sheets, text, journaling, and a painted map.

These are examples of a composition quilt (left) and a travel journal quilt (right).

# Color

Why stick to realistic colors when you have the whole rainbow to play with? I love exaggerating or changing colors to achieve a certain mood.

There are whole books devoted just to color and color theory. Reading these can be quite a long process. When I think about how I use color, I like to keep things simple. While I was attending art college in the 1980s, I attended a lecture by Kaffe Fassett about color and design. His bold use of color and pattern continues to influence my work to this day. My college friends and I were big knitters, and we would combine many balls of wool together into one sweater. Today I do not shy away from color and continue to choose bold fabrics for quilting projects.

Many of us are intimidated when choosing colors for a quilt. If you pull a variety of fabrics together and they don't jell, then something probably isn't right. You could start by removing any fabrics that shout out to you or limit your color choices to help guide you in the right direction.

Before choosing fabrics, I first think about what I am trying to achieve. Am I going for bright, primary colors or jewel tones with a high intensity? Or something more subtle, with tints in pastel or subdued tones? Or shades that are darker and more muted? How about complementary colors: red and green, blue and orange, or purple and yellow. I could use an analogous range of colors: blue/green/yellow, red/purple/blue, or red/orange/yellow. The color wheel is arranged by temperature, cool colors opposite warm colors. There are other color schemes like triadic and split complementary that you could also try, but I find it easier to keep things simple. It helps to keep within

# Let's Talk Color Basics

- **Primary colors:** Red, blue, and yellow
- **Secondary colors: Purple, green, and orange**
- **Value:** How light or dark the color is
- **Shade:** Color with black added
- **Tint:** Color with white added
- **Intensity:** How dull or bright the color is
- **Temperature:** Warm (red, orange, yellow) or cool (green, blue, purple)
- **Complementary colors:** Those opposite each other in the color wheel (e.g., red and green)
- **Analogous colors:** Those next to each other in the color wheel (e.g., red and orange)

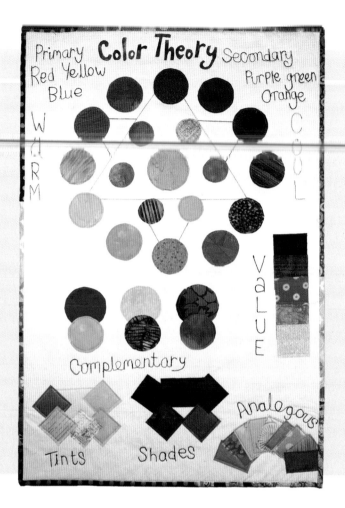

one of these parameters when making your fabric selections.

## NATURAL OR REALISTIC COLOR SCHEME

If I am making a pet portrait, for example, I will work with a realistic color scheme and try to make the pet look as it does in real life. When looking at your photo, you will be attempting to copy the colors you see. This removes much of the indecision in choosing colors. Your photo will be your color guide for the collage. When choosing fabrics, I recommend gathering more than you think you'll need. These will include all the values (dark, medium, and light). Don't be afraid to include some unexpected fabrics to create variety and texture.

## ABSTRACT COLOR SCHEME

If you are choosing an abstract or unconventional color scheme, the possibilities are endless, but you can easily be overwhelmed with choices. This is when I would choose

**Note the variety of gray fabrics used in this quilt. This captures the gradient of shadows, fur color, and fur texture on Marley in a realistic way.**

# Tip

Exaggerate what you see for more interest, adding more contrast from dark to light values.

This piece uses a limited color palette of muted cool tones. By following the shadows and highlights of the image, even unrealistic colors can look correct.

For Ruby, I used a fussy cut flower from a printed fabric in the center of the forehead. All my other colors came from this starting point.

a recognized color scheme as my guide or parameter, e.g., choosing a complementary color scheme like purple and yellow. If I am looking to create a tranquil-feeling quilt, I might choose a cool range of colors, but if I want to create something with energy, I would go for warm or analogous colors. By setting yourself some guidelines, or looking at colors in a narrower field on the color wheel, it will make choosing fabric easier.

## FOCUS FABRIC

There are so many wonderful quilting fabrics available that, sometimes, choosing just one fabric as the "focus fabric" can be the guide and inspiration you need. If it is a print or patterned, I will gather other fabrics related to what I see in that print.

I created this piece based on a photo I took in a restaurant called Hazel in Occidental, California.

# Finding the Perfect Photo or Image

Choosing a great photo is fundamental to making a great collage quilt. Luckily, today, we almost always have a phone on hand that takes great quality photos when inspiration strikes. I take many photographs that inspire ideas for use in a quilt. Sometimes, it can just be one element from that photo I use for my quilt design, or when working on a themed quilt, I might combine elements from several photos. You probably have plenty of great ideas and photos ready to use in your next project.

Photos are not the only source of ideas to use when designing your pattern for fabric collage. From photo apps to coloring books, and clip art to vintage illustrations, there is plenty of inspiration out there. I know not everyone can simply draw their design to use as a pattern, so I am hoping the instructions in this book will give you the tools to approach these projects with new enthusiasm and confidence.

## Copyright

You can find all kinds of photos on websites such as Instagram or Pinterest. I often see an image and think, "That would make a great quilt!" However, copyright can be an issue if you wish to share your quilt online, enter it into a quilt show, or be featured in a magazine. You need to receive the photographer's permission to use their photo. It may be as simple as messaging a person on social media and asking, "Can I use your photo as inspiration in my quilt?" You should offer to provide them with credit for the image. They may be willing to give you that permission and enjoy the exposure they will get in kind from your work. Sometimes you may have to pay a fee for its use. Often, it is easier to use your own photos or photos from a friend or relative.

PHOTO BY TANYA JAYNES

Flossie photo found on Pinterest. Permission given by owner.

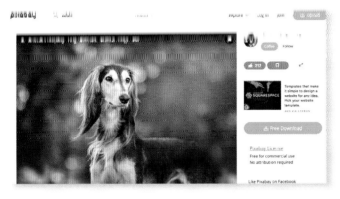

A stock photo website typically looks like this (above). After downloading the image, I cropped it and turned it into a collage quilt (right).

Depending on the subject matter, you might find that you do not have photos of the subjects you need. In these cases, I head to copyright-free websites. Here are some websites to consider: Pixabay, Unsplash, StockSnap, Pexels, FreeImages, and Shopify. By entering the subject matter into the search box, an array of results will pop up. If you use one of these, it is still courtesy to credit the photographer if you use their photo. For many of the themes in this book, I didn't have my own photograph and used Pixabay. I like to credit Pixabay.com and the photographer when I share information about the quilt. Copyright-free clip art is available online and offers simplified designs. On Facebook, there are many groups you can join where people share their own copyright-free photos, such as Free Artist Reference Photos, Free Animal Reference Photos for Artists, and Landscape Reference Photos for Artists.

The original drawing (left) gave me a lot of inspiration for a quilt (right). This style gives you permission to try new techniques that can result in something magical!

## Other Sources for Images

Here are some other sources for inspiration that might not occur to you right away, but make for some truly unique projects.

### CHILDREN'S ARTWORK

I have been known to use my children's artwork from elementary or preschool in quilts. The images and themes they come up with are innocent, charming, unexpected, and totally unique! Using this type of design gives you permission to work more freely, just a child does. They also make great gifts!

## COLORING BOOKS

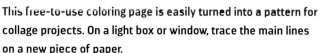

This free-to-use coloring page is easily turned into a pattern for collage projects. On a light box or window, trace the main lines on a new piece of paper.

When starting a fabric collage, you essentially need a line drawing. You can create your own from a photograph, but another great source for finding these are in coloring books. You could use the image as is, enlarge it, or combine it with other images for your collage. I signed up for the Dover Publishing newsletter and am sent a weekly selection of free coloring pages I can download. So long as you are not reprinting and distributing these pages, you can use them for free. What I like to do is print the page, take a permanent marker, and trace over parts of the image to create a thicker line, ignoring many of the smaller details for a simplified design. I can then enlarge the image to the size required for my fabric collage.

   **Important note:** Even though these pages are free to use, you still should not claim the piece as your own. You should give credit if posting online. Seek permission if showing in a gallery, contest, or selling.

### PHOTOS OR ILLUSTRATIONS IN THE PUBLIC DOMAIN

Every year, January 1st is Public Domain Day. This means copyrighted materials from a particular year are released and can be accessed by the public. Any materials prior to that year are also available. Once these images are in the public domain, you can incorporate them into your work. In 2022, works from 1926 were released and the first *Winnie-the-Pooh* book by A. A. Milne became available. Search on Public Domain Day for the latest works available in the US. For collage, useful images or materials are book covers, book illustrations, and movie posters.

## VINTAGE DRAWINGS AND ILLUSTRATIONS

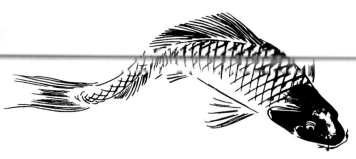

Free download from the Heritage Type website.

Many websites offer free vintage illustrations that are suitable for collage. Once the illustration becomes old enough and enters the public domain, the image is available for artists to incorporate into their artwork. If you search for free downloads through Heritage Type Co., hundreds of images are available. You can find almost anything, from birds, people, plants, under the sea, and more. These can be used to create your pattern or part of your pattern.

### OTHER SOURCES I USE

Photo editing apps can be helpful to change or manipulate your photos to achieve a different look. Many are free for a limited version, or you can buy the app to access all their features. I experiment with a couple of these apps, including Waterlogue, Painnt, and Vector Q. Select a filter for the image and the app will simplify the colors and shapes, making it easier to draw your pattern. This new image can be printed out as the source for your pattern.

Photo of my sister-in-law's Burmese kittens (left), and the same image adjusted using the Waterlogue application (right).

## What Makes a Great Photo

If you have a photo that you are intuitively drawn to, it's probably a good candidate for use in your project. This excitement will encourage you to take the design process further. Good lighting, good contrast, and good coloring are key. Ensuring your photo has good lighting is important as this will create more contrast; you will see more colors or areas that will translate to a variety of colored fabrics in the collage process. If the photo is too dark, it will be hard to define different areas and you will have to figure them out yourself. If you edit the photo with a filter to increase the lighting and contrast, this will help.

If you are using an animal photo as your inspiration for the quilt, having them looking straight at the camera is great as you really focus on the details of the eyes. A nice profile shot is also good as you can see the shape of the head. A close-up can also be fun as the foreshortened image will change the proportions and can be quite comical.

Starting from top left: Original Ziggy photo, cropped photo, cropped with a vivid filter applied, and cropped with a monotone filter applied.

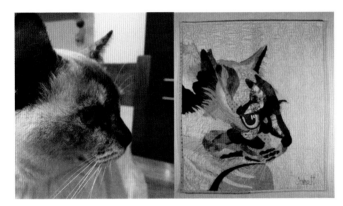

This picture of Tilly's profile shows off the eye (left), which makes for a captivating quilt (right).

## Let's Talk Value

Part of the pattern-making process is drawing shapes to define where different fabrics will be used. You need to observe where the values change to determine where those shapes are, so it's best to keep that in mind while taking and choosing your photos. I think of value as contrast; in collage, you need contrast for a more successful quilt. It is the contrast that creates dimension.

### VALUE = CONTRAST = DIMENSION

When it comes to using fabrics: use dark fabrics in the shadow areas where less light is reaching, use medium fabrics across much of your collage, and use light fabrics in the highlights or where the light source will be hitting. Of course, when referencing colors in a photo, use colors relative to what you see.

## Preparing the Photo for Printing

There is a lot of unnecessary background in the original photo that won't be used (left). Cropping puts the focus all on Poppy.

If your photo includes extra, unnecessary background, you need to crop, cut, or remove this so your subject is all that remains. If you cut a physical photo to resize, reprint this smaller photo by selecting "fit to page" on your printer so it fills that letter-size page. Print out as an 8" x 10" (20.3 x 25.4cm) photo. If you cropped the image on your computer, save the cropped image at 8" x 10" (20.3 x 25.4cm) or full page and print out. Cropping will make your image and its details as large as they can be before the next step of making the pattern.

I like to print out one copy in color and one in black and white. I will use the color one to draw or trace over for the pattern; the black and white one is reference when looking at values and when making the collage.

Now you have the design for your collage, whether it's a photo, clip art, coloring page, or vintage illustration. And you know how to resize it. Now it's time to make the pattern. This is a fun time in the design process. Get excited about this new project as you consider the color palette and fabrics you will use.

# Creating the Pattern

Now you have your photo or image selected, cropped, and printed, the next step is the drawing stage! This part can feel hard, and you may feel fearful. Many students find drawing intimidating as it's not something they do on a daily basis. But you should relax. This is a short process before you get to the fun part: playing with fabric.

To make the pattern, you will be dividing the photo up into different areas or shapes. Although you are drawing on top of a photo, you are basically making a line drawing. Remember each shape will be cut out in a different fabric. Think about it like a coloring book page, where you would add color into various sections. For this lesson, I am going to use a photograph of my hiking boots as an example.

## Pattern Drawing Tips

Make sure that you focus on these areas:

- Draw the outline.

- Draw where the colors change.

- Draw where the values change.

- Draw shadows and highlights.

- Draw shapes for different colors and values, looking for dark, medium, and light areas.

- For people and animals, draw lines that follow the contours on the face or the direction of the fur.

## Tip

Before you begin, spend five minutes looking at your color photo. Really study it. You will begin to see areas where the color changes, areas that are dark or light, and shadows and highlights. You can think about where you would use different colors or values of fabric.

### SUPPLIES

- 8" x 10" (20.3 x 25.4cm) photo in color
- 8" x 10" (20.3 x 25.4cm) photo in black and white
- 8½" x 11" (21.6 x 27.9cm) tracing paper
- Lightbox or a sunny window
- Pencil
- Fine black permanent marker
- Copier, scanner, and printer
- Painter's or masking tape

## Making the Line Drawing

PHOTO CREDIT: JAMES HAWORTH

**1. Lay the color photo on your light box.** Layer the tracing paper on top and secure with tape. If using a window, tape the photo and tracing paper in a sunny spot. Using a light box or a window is necessary because the light projects through the photo onto your paper; the illumination enables you to draw.

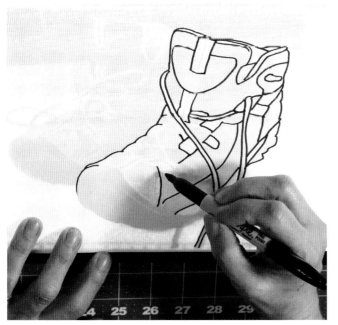

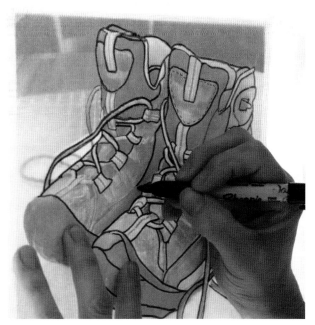

**2. Trace the lines with permanent marker.** Draw with confidence and keep the lines smooth. If you are a little unsure, begin by using a pencil. I like to use a fine-tip pen, but if there is a lot of small detail, I'll use an ultra-fine-tip pen. Don't draw every little line as the pattern will become overwhelming and overcomplicated. Keep the drawing relatively simple and remember this is just a guide. The small details can be added later using fabric.

**3. Make your lines meet others to form enclosed shapes.** Keep this in mind as you are drawing. Remember each shape will be a piece of fabric that you will cut out and when the pattern is enlarged the shapes will be larger.

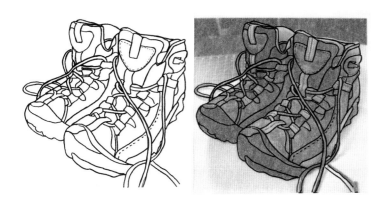

**4. Remove the paper layer from the photograph.** Connect any lines that are not joined to form shapes. If you drew in pencil, now you can confidently draw your pattern with the marker. If you used vellum or tracing paper, photocopy your design onto copy paper.

## Drawing Hair and Fur

When drawing the fur of a very hairy animal or pet, I do not draw every strand of hair or fluffy area. There would just be too many small and thin details to cut out. I draw a gentle zigzag or point to suggest the fur. If I want to show a lot of fine hair, I will use my sewing machine for a stitch line to portray this detail. I discuss this more in Guide to Making Animals and Pets (page 40).

# Enlarging the Pattern

Now that your line drawing or pattern is on a regular piece of copy paper, there are a number of options to use to make this larger and ready for collage. Consider what size quilt you will make. The finished piece will be larger once the background is added, so remember the enlargement is for the focal image size only. When working on my collage process I work on a horizontal tabletop, not a design wall, so I take that into consideration.

When teaching, I suggest a 200% enlargement as it fits nicely on a tabletop and is a convenient size. The larger the enlargement, the larger your pieces will be. Saying that, the smaller the image, the smaller the fabric pieces will be—and they can get really small!

Here is a good rule of thumb:

- 200% for approximately 16" x 20" (40.6 x 50.8cm) image
- 250% for approximately 20" x 26" (50.8 x 66cm) image
- 300% for approximately 24" x 30" (61 x 76.2cm) image

At the back of the book, you will find the patterns I made for some of the projects in this book. Where appropriate, I listed the size I used to make the enlargement. If not stated, the pattern is used at the same size. As part of my desire for you to work creatively, you have my permission to enlarge these patterns to whatever size you need and use the collage you make however you wish. I suggest photocopying the patterns from this book, saving them as JPEG or PDF files on your computer, then enlarging and printing them for your unique design or project.

## Tip

Once you have your enlarged image on paper, remember this will be your pattern, so don't be afraid to write on it. Mark it up with obvious colors, and note the areas that are the darkest and the lightest. It can be useful to draw small arrows to mark where a piece will tuck under another as part of the layering process. This will be covered more in Learning to Collage (page 32).

## FIVE METHODS OF ENLARGEMENT

You can choose whichever method you feel most comfortable doing to make your enlargement. It is always nice once this step is complete so you can move onto choosing and playing with color and fabrics.

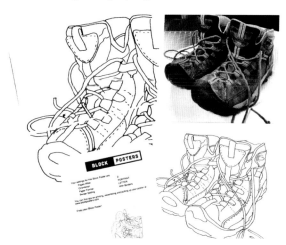

My hiking boots printed over four sheets at two pages wide, approximately 200% enlargement.

**1.** Scan your pattern on your all-in-one printer at home. Save this file either as a PDF or JPEG file on your computer. Upload the JPEG file to a website designed for this type of printing, such as Block Posters. Here you choose the enlargement size by selecting how many papers wide you need. You can also change the orientation to either portrait or landscape. It will show the finished dimensions and how many papers it will print onto. Once printed, you will need to trim the papers and tape them together.

**2.** Take your paper pattern or your scanned image on a memory stick to your local print shop or office supply store and ask them to enlarge it for you on their large format printer. Tell them the percentage size that you require. They should print it on blueprint paper, and it should be inexpensive.

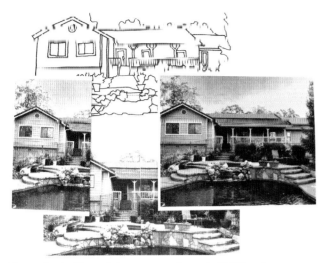

This method will result in an approximately 150% enlargement.

**3.** Try using the enlargement feature on your copier/printer. Print out an 8" x 10" (20.3 x 25.4cm) photo. Fold this photo in half and lay it onto the bed of the copier. Select "Fit to Page," which will print that half image onto a full page. Turn the folded photo over and repeat. Tape these two pages together for an image measuring 11" x 14" (27.9 x 35.6cm). Trace the lines needed onto a new piece of paper.

For this drawing, an enlargement of 250% will print onto nine pages.

**4.** Another method to print at home is to open your PDF image in the application Adobe Acrobat Reader. Go to file and select "Print." On the print window, click the "Poster" button. Here you will be able to adjust the Tile Scale. It will be at 100%, but by changing it to 200% or larger and selecting "Poster" again, you will see how many pages it will print on. By changing the portrait or landscape orientation, it may print more efficiently. Once printed, you will need to trim the papers and tape them together. I cannot guarantee that everyone's computer works like mine, so this method may not work for you.

**5.** The grid-to-grid technique (instructions follow).

## GRID-TO-GRID TECHNIQUE

The Bed-Size Maxi Quilt (page 124) was enlarged at 500%. If I had printed this out as a PDF on my printer at home, it would have been 35 pages. To enlarge the pattern, I decided I would use the old-fashioned grid-to-grid technique. I have done this previously when making large quilts as I cannot imagine trying to trim and tape together a huge number of pages.

After creating the line drawing, I put the pattern behind a grid.

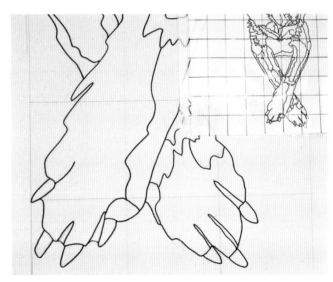

Draw a larger grid on a large sheet of paper. Then match the lines shown in the small grid to the large grid.

This technique involves putting the small pattern behind a 1" (2.5cm) grid. I used a clear page protector with a 1" (2.5cm) grid drawn with a permanent black marker. Next, I transferred the details in each square onto a corresponding square in a 5" (12.7cm) grid I had drawn on a large piece of paper. This results in 500% enlargement.

# chapter 2

# Techniques

## Learning to Collage

There are various methods of fabric collage. Raw-edge collage is a type of appliqué. Appliqué is a form of ornamentation where a cut-out design is sewn or applied to a piece of material. In raw-edge collage, the edge of the fabric is included, and you are not turning or hiding that edge. You just cut out the piece you need and that's it! The result has a different look compared to other methods of appliqué, like needle-turn. By doing this, I feel as if I am cheating in a way, because it looks just as good with much less work.

One method of assembling collage is to use a fusible product on the back of the fabric; this makes the piece tacky and able to be repositioned before finding the right spot and ironing down. I don't use this technique as I like the immediacy of being able to pick and choose any of my fabrics (from my whole stash!) without fusing them first. Plus, this would use a lot of fusible product, and layers of fusible can make the collage stiff and harder to stitch through. Although I layer my fabrics (having up to five layers!), I never have a problem stitching through them. The resulting quilt is still soft and has a drape. This would not be the case if five fused layers were used.

**Fabric collage is easier with a large selection of fabrics.**

My technique is free form. I gather a large pile of fabrics, select which to use, and cut as much or as little as required. I layer my pieces, and when I am happy with their positioning, I will hold them in place with a little glue. You don't need too much glue as the pieces will be stitched later to secure them. The stitching allows you to add more detail and creates texture.

I think of fabric collage like paper collage—you are cutting, layering, and gluing into place. Remember, because we are working with raw edges and no fusible, some fabrics may fray. This might not be a look that you like. I don't mind it, although quilt show judges have criticized my work for this in the past. I just go for it! I mostly make wall hangings, so washing a piece isn't something I worry about. I have washed my quilts to see what happens, and I didn't see a noticeable difference in the quality or appearance. "Embrace the fray" and have fun!

# Cutting the Collage

These are the basic steps I use for the majority of my collage projects. In these instructions I will be referencing the hummingbird pattern found on page 142. I enlarged the pattern at 225% and taped the 4 printed pages of the larger bird together. For this example, I then traced the bird onto a single piece of paper but this step is not necessary.

## Tip

If your fabric is crinkled, folded, or bumpy, it is worth pressing it under an iron. This will make tracing easier.

### SUPPLIES

- Pattern
- 8" x 10" (20.3 x 25.4cm) photo in color
- 8" x 10" (20.3 x 25.4cm) photo in black and white
- Selection of fabrics
- Interfacing or stabilizer for foundation (I used Pellon 830 Easy Pattern)
- Collage supplies (page 13)
- Painter's tape
- Tweezers
- Lightbox (optional)

### INSTRUCTIONS

**1. Lay the foundation over the pattern.** Use painter's tape to secure these together in a couple of places. You need to be able to see the dark lines through the foundation. This is what the fabrics get glued onto. If you will be using a light box, lay it under the pattern.

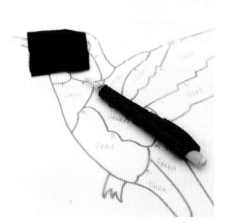

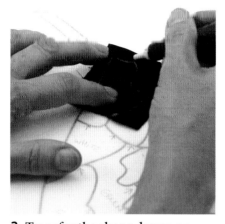

**2. Start in a focus area, such as the head, flower center, or eyes.** Select the shape to cut and fabric to use. I chose the large, black head piece. If necessary, cut down the fabric so it's a similar size to the shape. Lay the fabric piece over the shape to be traced.

**3. Transfer the shape drawn on the pattern to the top of the fabric.** Remember it does not need to be totally accurate. If you are using a light box and a light-colored fabric, the line will show through your fabric. If neither apply, lift the fabric slightly, spot the line, and draw a dash or line on the fabric with your marker. Your drawn line can be hard to see depending on the fabric, so either join up the line or darken it so you can see it. Repeat this process around the shape until you have a complete sketch.

**4. Cut the shape out.** Lay the piece onto the pattern and see how you did! It does not have to be exact as there is a lot of forgiveness in this technique, so give yourself a break. Repeat. Continue to choose fabrics, draw, and cut the shapes, layering as you go.

## Layering Your Fabrics is a Fundamental Part of Collage

Fabrics need to layer over other fabrics either with an overlap of approximately ¼" (6mm) allowance, which is where the glue is applied, or simply laid on top. I draw small arrows on the foundation to indicate where one fabric needs to extend under another piece of fabric.

How do I know which layer is on top? In nature, whatever is closest to you appears on top. In appliqué, people layer this way, and in collage, this is what we are doing also. In this example project, the wings lay over the hummingbird's body and tail, the beak goes behind the head, and the feet tuck under the body. The more you work with collage, the more this method will become familiar to you. If you have the layers positioned incorrectly, they will look wrong or unnatural.

Mark arrows on the pattern to remind you where that ¼" (6mm) extra fabric needs to be added. As you cut and do more collage, these steps will become second nature.

## ADDING THE SEAM ALLOWANCE FOR LAYERING

When an overlap or seam allowance is needed for layering, there are a couple of ways to do this:

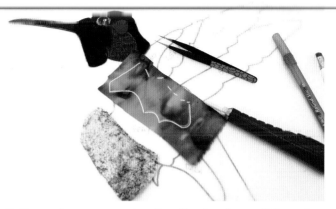

**1. Lay the edge of your chosen fabric with a ¼"** (6mm) **overlap where it will be tucked under.** You don't need to cut this edge. Ignore this edge, but draw the exact cutting line for the rest of the shape.

**2. Draw the exact cutting line for the shape.** Where the overlap will be, mark with a dashed line adding on the ¼" (6mm) allowance. This will be your cutting line.

## Gluing the Collage

**1. Glue when you have several cut pieces layered on the pattern.** Make sure you are happy with your fabric choices. Apply glue between the layers and press down using your finger. Early in the collage process, only apply a little glue. This will make the layers easier to pull apart in case you need to move a piece or add a layer.

**2. Keep the shapes in the correct place as you build your collage.** Fix your collage to the foundation by adding a little glue under the center of the piece. Remember to keep the edges free of glue so layers can slide underneath.

## Tip

This is not a photorealistic technique. Its forgiving nature allows for variations from the original pattern. When the pattern is removed, nobody knows what lines you were following. Remember it's supposed to be FUN!

**3. Continue gluing where the layers overlap.** As you build up your collage by gluing the layers together, the glue will secure to the foundation. I like to cut many pieces until I feel happy with the result, then add the glue. Continue to choose fabrics, cut, and glue.

**4. When the collage is complete, check that all the layers are glued.** Do this before stitching, otherwise the layers might catch around the needle as you stitch. Cut away the excess foundation so you have a single unit of collage with the trimmed foundation on the back. For small collaged pieces or thin details, like a flower stalk or the bird's beak, I don't include a layer of foundation behind them.

## Fussy or Free-Cutting Collage

Not all the cut pieces need to be traced. Small details that lay on top of a piece of fabric are fussy cut or free-cut.

- **Fussy cutting** is when you deliberately cut a piece of fabric to showcase a picture or print within it. These pieces are usually cut from large-scale or novelty prints. I like to look for text or words on selvages to include in my collage.

This hummingbird has more details free-cut and layered on.

- **Free-cutting** is when you eyeball or estimate a shape to cut from a fabric. In the hummingbird collage, I free-cut small feather shapes to add more interest.

- Use your **off-cuts** (leftover fabric) as you are working for small or additional details.

These butterflies were fussy cut from one piece of fabric.

# Thinking About Fabric

Here is another example of collage, showing the process of making my hiking boots. Finding the right values in my fabric choices here was important. I tried to find fabric colors similar to the real boots. Once you begin choosing fabrics and working on building the collage, you will relax and have fun. Don't spend too long making fabric choices, as this can be very time consuming. Choose one and move along. In the big picture, this fabric will just be a small detail in that collage. If it stands out as wrong, remove it or lay a different fabric over the top to fix.

Remember, more fabrics will add to the serendipitous nature of collage and keep it interesting and colorful. We are only using little bits of fabric, and I am sure you have plenty to choose from in your stash!

**1. Choose fabrics that work with colors and textures in the boots.** I initially planned to include red, then made that an accent color. Place foundation over the pattern.

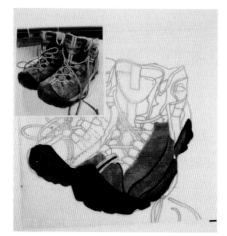

**2. Start with the large dark rubber toe pieces.** Since this area is the closest to the camera, it will be on top of the other fabric pieces. Then create the sole of the first boot.

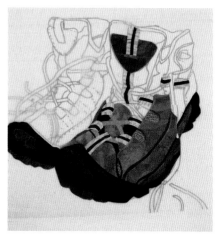

**3. Make the laces and striped lace loops.** Look for good contrast so each piece is distinct in the whole collage.

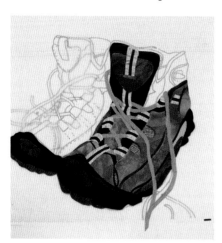

**4. Work on the laces and tongue of the boot.** While the strings don't exactly match the pattern, it's okay to deviate if you think it will look better.

**5. Construct the second boot.** Make sure to create contrast between the two boots so they don't merge together.

**6. Make sure everything is glued down.** Cut away the excess foundation, and preview the collage piece on various backgrounds.

# More Tips When Making a Collage

- When starting a collage, I **begin with a focus area** (usually in the center) and work out from there.

- If you are working on **an area that covers adjacent shapes**, cut some of the pieces, set them aside, then cut the shapes that were obscured or covered. Once all the pieces are cut, bring them back, position the layers, and glue.

- If you have mainly used large pieces of fabric and the resulting collage looks flat, **create more texture by free-cutting** some extra layers. This will help add more dimension.

- If you just need an **echo or small border** around a piece, hold your fabric shape over a contrast fabric and trim around the piece, leaving a small shadow. You can glue the two pieces together before cutting.

- **Use your glue sparingly**. Don't glue down around the edges as you will likely need to layer or tuck a piece underneath.

- If you **cut your shape too small**, cut an additional piece in the same fabric, layer in place, and glue. Using a curved line will blend and not be noticed.

- If you find a **small hole between shapes**, cut a small piece of the same fabric, and use it to fill the hole or layer it on top of the hole. Glue in place.

- For small designs, like flowers and leaves, **don't use a foundation** behind them. Glue fabric to fabric.

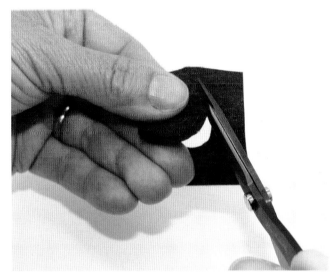

You don't need to cut very wide when creating a border or "echo." Even a little will make the piece pop.

- **Small details and lines** can be included through stitching. For example, fence details on a house or whiskers on a cat.

- **Take photos as you go** as the image in the camera is reduced and flattened. You will see your collage in a new perspective.

- **Stand up and take a break**! It's good to stretch and not stay sitting for hours on end. This technique is quite addictive.

- If you spend too long focused on a small area, you may forget to **look at the whole design**. Taking a break helps here too.

# Guide to Making Animals and Pets

Photo reference is invaluable when recreating animals. Small details turn a regular dog into your pet!

When I started teaching my collage technique, I quickly realized that, rather than using one of my premade animal patterns, students had a desire to make unique quilts of their own pets. I changed the structure of my lesson so students could bring in an enlarged photograph to make their individual pet pattern for collaging.

Making something more personal means you are more invested in the project and its outcome. These finished quilts become family treasures, either for oneself or to give as a gift. I love when everyone in my class is able to share unique photographs and stories about furry family members. Often, pets that are no longer around are memorialized in these quilts, which can stir up a lot of emotions.

Here, I want to share a few tips about how I make my animal or pet collages. Over the years, I have created many custom pet portraits for clients, so I hope to share what I have learned to make the process easier and more successful for you. The basic collage technique will be the same as the previous chapter, but I will go more in depth about making the pattern, realistic eyes, a simple nose, and tips for making and stitching fur.

Here, I am picking out the detail of the striped fur and the dark shading around the eyes of the cat. I am thinking about where I would use different fabric colors.

In this pattern, I have darkened the lines between the dark and light fur and marked the pattern to indicate the dark areas.

## Drawing the Pattern

When drawing the outline of a very furry animal, it can be hard to see the edge of the fur. However, you will need to draw a defined edge or outline for the animal. So, rather than marking every spike or piece of fur, I generalize these with a smooth or gently rounded zigzag shape. If you add every piece of fur, these fine lines will be impossible to cut out. Remember, you will be able to include more detailed fur using stitching lines.

When tracing the pattern of a photo of an animal with dark fur, it can be hard to see any definition between areas in a photograph. You can try using a filter on the photo before printing it out to hopefully create more contrast. Then draw on the photo using a silver, white, or regular pencil and divide up the area following the direction of the fur.

When working with a light-colored animal, it can be hard to see a lot of variation in the fur color. Look closely for shadows between the fur, exaggerate what you see, and include all kinds of white, gray, yellow, pink, and light blue fabrics. For a dark-colored animal, use an assortment of black fabrics in different values to add variety and divide up those large dark areas of fur that appear to be the same color.

When I create the eyes, I use several circles of fabric to define the different colors and areas. This creates depth. When tracing over the photo to create your pattern, the eyes will be too small to draw in all these details,

It's easier to add extra colors to your collage during the fabric cutting process; drawing too many details on the pattern can become confusing.

but they can be added once you start cutting out your fabrics. Remember the pattern is a guide that you have permission to change once working in fabrics.

I do not draw the whiskers onto the pattern. I will add these with stitching at the end.

# Making the Eyes

I encourage you to start with the eyes. The eyes are the most important part of making a pet or animal portrait, ~~so if you can get this right, you are well on your way to~~ a rewarding fabric portrait. Although they are more fiddly, as the size of the pieces will be small and there should be many layers, making the eyes is worth the extra time. Without using a fusible product, you are still able to stitch through these layers, so don't get concerned. I often have as many as five or six layers and have no problems.

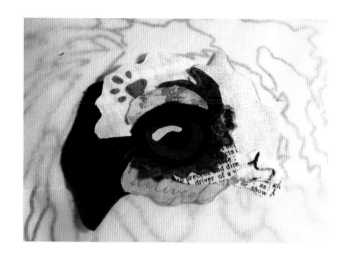

Every eye color, shape, and look are different, so your process may not look exactly like mine. These are the basic steps I generally use. Only when I am happy with my layered cut pieces will I glue my eye layers into a complete unit.

## Layers of the Eye

The eyes are made up of a number of layered circles, ovals, or half circles. It's useful to know the various parts so you can achieve a realistic look. Once the eyes are made and the animal is "looking back at you," you will be happy and more invested in finishing the project.

- **Pupil.** Black or dark circle at the center of the eye.
- **Iris.** This is the color that surrounds the pupil. Try to include two different colored fabrics (these will be two layers). Look for batiks or mottled fabrics rather than a solid color. Look closely at the iris as it may have a dark rim or edge. Cat eyes are very striking, so finding the right colors and fabrics is important to create that visual appeal.
- **Highlight or catchlight.** White or light fabric creates the light reflecting off the eyeball. It is very important to include the highlight as it brings life and realism to the eye. These will usually be on the same place on each eye, reflecting from a light source.
- **Shadow under the eyelid.** This is a darker part of the iris. You may notice this in the photograph, but if the eye is small, it might be too hard to include.

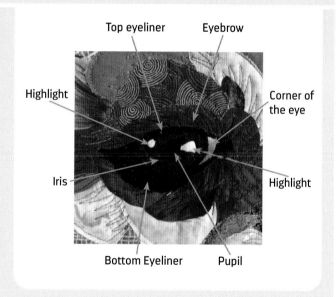

- **Corners of the eye.** Depending on the eye shape you may need to fill these in with small triangles of a light, white, or pink fabric.
- **Eyeliner.** I usually include a thin line of dark or black fabric to surround the eye. This helps define and set off the eye, rather like how humans apply eyeliner. This layer can be around the whole iris, around the bottom of the eye, or as a black edge to the eyelid.

# INSTRUCTIONS

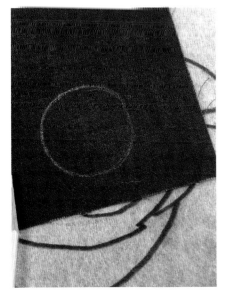

**1.** **Draw the iris onto the fabric.** When cutting the fabric for the iris, remember the top of the eye will be covered by an eyelid and eyebrow. Make the fabric large enough so the eyelid can layer over without covering the iris completely. Cut out.

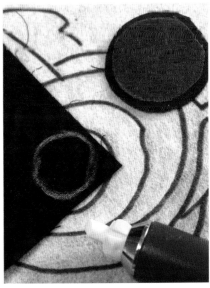

**2.** **Echo the iris with a dark fabric.** This creates an extra ring around the iris that is evident in some eyes; this is separate from the eyeliner. Cut a small black pupil.

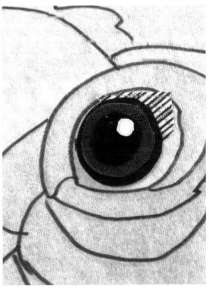

**3.** **Cut the highlight.** Layer the parts of the eye, adjusting as needed. Fill in the eye corners with triangles of fabric.

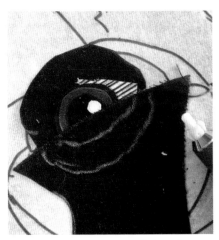

**4.** **Cut a black "eyeliner" for above and below the eye.** This may be difficult to see or not be visible in some photos. Most of this will be covered by next piece of fabric.

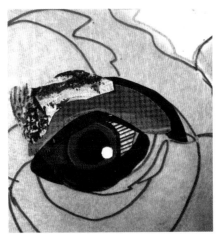

**5.** **Cut the eyelid, eyebrow, and detail layers.** This will enclose the eye, creating the illusion of the eye socket. The eye is a transition area for layering your collage fabrics. Fabrics cut after the eyebrow will be tucked under as they go away from the face toward the top of the head. Fabrics below the eye will be tucked under the eye, going toward the nose and mouth.

**6.** **Continue to add layers around the eye.** Once the eyeball and eyelid are complete, look at your original photo for areas of color and texture around the eye. This is a good opportunity to include a nice variety of colored and patterned fabrics.

When making animal quilts, I imagine stroking the animal in the direction of the fur. You would never stroke it "against the fur." The same applies to layering the fabrics. As your hand moves front to back, the layers will be tucked under the one on top, so you are never brushing into the raw edge of the fabric.

### CAT EYES

Cats typically have larger eyes than dogs, when compared to the size of their head. When making their eyes, you have more opportunities to play with color and texture to create visual appeal.

**Multiple layers of fabric come together to create an eye with a lot of depth and visual interest.**

This cat's eye shape is a large half oval with a dark eyelid covering the top of the eye. When cutting layers for the eye, I extended the fabric at the top (adding seam allowance), and then used the eyelid to cover and enclose the eye. A narrow black eyeliner goes around the bottom of the eye.

This cat's eye has three different blue-green colors for the iris, a black and dark gray for the pupil, and three very light blues for the highlight. As this eye is large, about 3" (7.6cm), I was able to include a variety of fabrics. I enclosed it with a dark brown eyelid and the black eyeliner around the bottom of the eye.

# Making the Nose

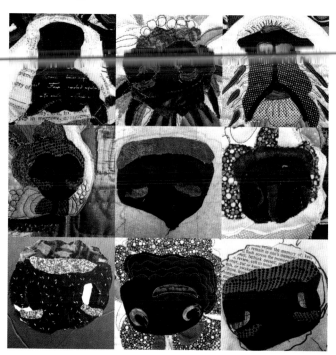

**While noses can look very different from one another, breaking them into simple shapes can make it easy to simplify and collage them.**

If you look at how noses are portrayed in art, it is often just a small line, a couple of nostrils, or a shadow that conveys where the nose is located on the face. If you look at a real nose or snout, they are a complicated combination of curves, shadows, lines, and holes. When making a nose, don't overwork or overthink it. If possible, find a fabric that has pattern or texture that can do the work for you. Remember, every nose is different, and cat noses are simpler than dog noses.

## Tip

You may be thinking, "Noses can be tricky!" My remedy is to keep things *simple*.

## CAT NOSE

**1. Choose your fabric, probably a pink.** Trace and cut out the small triangle shape. Include the indents for the nostrils.

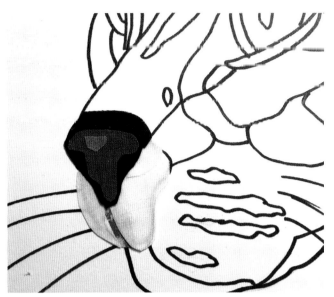

**2. Hold this nose to a dark or black fabric.** Trim around, leaving a small outline. Cutting this as a triangle shape will create the dark nostrils where the indents are. Include a highlight if needed. Glue the layers together.

## DOG NOSE

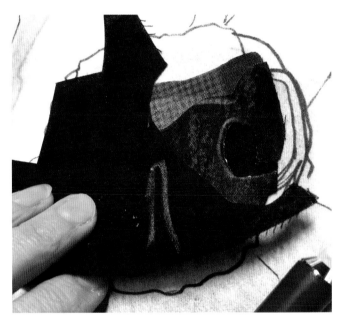

**1. Choose a suitable fabric, trace, and cut the main nose shape.** To create dark nostrils, first mark and cut out circles from this initial fabric piece. Cut in from the edge of the fabric. Create two small black fabric circles to glue behind the holes, reminiscent of "reverse appliqué." Add a narrow dark line of fabric on the bottom-center nose. Glue these layers together.

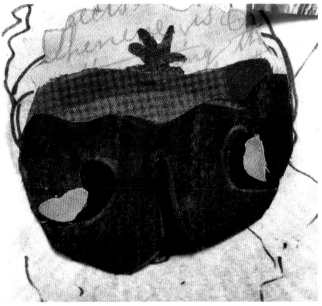

**2. Include a light highlight or reflection near the nostrils.** Here, I used a pink fabric. Add a light fabric highlight near the top of the nose. Include some transition fabric, as the nose moves from skin to fur, at the top of the nose. Glue.

# More Tips for Animal Collage

- **The order for making a pet portrait**: the eyes, the area around the eyes, the nose, then fill in between the two. Don't be afraid to cut a number of pieces first before committing to gluing.

- When the **eye layers are glued together** and are a complete unit (use the pattern as a guide), position them onto the foundation, and add a spot of glue under the center of each eye so they stay in the correct spot.

- **For a very furry animal**, cut larger areas in a single fabric. Then fussy cut the chunks of different-colored fur to layer over it.

- **The face will be the most detailed**. Working away from the collaged face to the neck and body, the collage becomes less detailed and the pieces are larger.

- When adding a detail like a collar, **choose a good contrast** to the fur so that it stands out. To create the crisp edge of a collar—rather than leaving it raw edge—fold the edge so it has more dimension.

## Tip

In collage, fabric is the first layer, and the stitching provides extra texture.

The collar on a pet shouldn't distract from the face, but it's important to choose something that will balance the piece as a whole.

# Stitching Tips

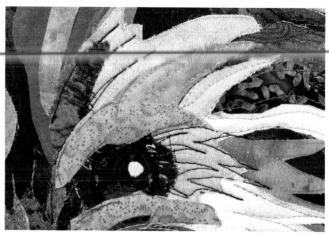

Using thread that contrasts to the fabric underneath makes the "hair" stand out and ties the different fabric colors together.

Once the collage is complete and free-cut details have been added, the focal point is glued to the background (page 51). After checking everything is secure, you will be ready to stitch. This will be discussed in more detail in Free-Motion Quilting for Collage (page 52), but I find that animals require unique instructions. For instance, fur texture is added with stitching. Here are some tips for making your animal collage as realistic as possible.

- **Use a variety of colored threads** that either blend or contrast with the fabrics to add more detail and interest. Include variegated threads, if you have them, as they are an easy way to include a mixture of colors.

- **Stitch out to a point** at the end of the fur to create that furry texture.

- **Only add whiskers when all the stitching is complete.** I usually use a 12wt thread to stitch up and back for each whisker or hand stitch with embroidery floss.

Every pet or animal collage that you make will bring new and different challenges. Think about the differences between making a long-haired animal versus a short, smooth-haired one. Remember these instructions are not for just making cat or dog faces; consider creating other animal collages. What fun would it be to recreate the wild, shaggy fur of a buffalo, the patterns of a big cat's coat, the texture of reptile skin, or the colorful feathers of parrots? Embrace the challenge and just give it a go.

# Choosing a Background

Choosing the right background is important. Background fabric (the fabric piece that the collage will be attached to) is not to be confused with backing fabric (fabric put on the back of the quilt as part of the three sandwich layers). Making the right choice can make or break the quilt. You have spent a lot of time creating the collage, so your background needs to complement, enhance, and contrast with the collage. You do not want it to become lost.

## Preparing the Collage

Now your collage is complete, there are a few things to do before adding a background.

**1. Check all the fabric pieces have been glued down.** Once your quilt is under the sewing machine, it is easy for fabric points to snag, fold, and get caught around the needle. Save yourself the hassle by checking now!

**2. Remove the paper pattern.** With the application of glue, it is likely that the foundation will be stuck to the pattern paper in places. If this happens, you just need to slide your hand between the two layers and gently separate them. If this is a problem, next time add a layer of parchment paper between the two layers as glue will not stick to this.

**3. Remove the excess foundation from around the collage.** The collage should not be glued around its outside edge. Cut using your scissors behind the

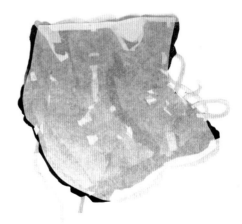

You just need to remove enough foundation so it doesn't show from the front.

edge of the collage. If it is glued around the edge, no worries—you will just need to be more careful when cutting. The goal is to have a single unit of collage with no foundation fabric showing on the front. This you can now confidently take and preview on different background choices.

# Color Choices for the Background

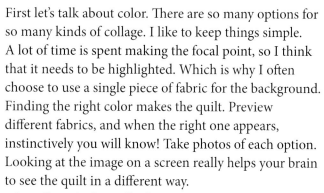

This mostly black and white dog made for a good opportunity to use a bold background.

A colorful focal point pairs well with a neutral background so the details aren't lost.

First let's talk about color. There are so many options for so many kinds of collage. I like to keep things simple. A lot of time is spent making the focal point, so I think that it needs to be highlighted. Which is why I often choose to use a single piece of fabric for the background. Finding the right color makes the quilt. Preview different fabrics, and when the right one appears, instinctively you will know! Take photos of each option. Looking at the image on a screen really helps your brain to see the quilt in a different way.

In collage, I often talk about creating contrast, and this is what to look for here. The piece needs to stand out from the background. A good first step is to look for a complementary color scheme. For example, if you have used realistic colors in an animal collage, you will have more options for a bright, colorful background. The opposite would be true if the collage is made using bold, abstract colors; for a background you could choose blacks, whites, or neutrals.

## Background Design Options

Consider your quilt as a whole: the collage combined with the background. When choosing the background, does your quilt have a theme or narrative you can work with? Also, it must not distract from the collage itself. You may already know what background fabric you wish to use, but here are some options I will discuss.

### ONE PIECE OF FABRIC

Often, I use one piece of fabric, as I like the focus to be on the collage. There are three choices here: solid, small print, or a large print.

**Solid colored fabric.** I often feel intimidated using a solid fabric for a background because your quilting stitch pattern will be on show. If you are an accomplished free-motion quilter, go ahead and use this space to show off your skills. For new or less confident quilters, I would avoid a solid fabric.

In this custom quilt, I used a silk fabric that the customer chose. I had to practice the stitch pattern first because I couldn't make any mistakes.

Some small print fabrics can almost trick the eye into looking solid because they aren't distracting from the subject.

This complementary-colored cat, using yellow and purple fabrics, is placed on a contrasting, large-motif print fabric.

**Small print or texture.** These are my go-to fabrics for backgrounds. Stitching on this fabric is less intimidating as the quilting pattern will blend away. By choosing a matching color thread, the stitching won't show; if you want it to stand out, use a contrasting color thread. Using a Moda Grunge tone-on-tone fabric, the variation adds interest without being distracting and visually looks like a single color. Batiks, hand-dyes, and ombre fabrics are also good choices.

**Large motif or print.** I love to use bold, unexpected prints in many of my pet portrait quilts. It's important to find the balance between it working and not being distracting. There are many great fabrics available; for example, the Kaffe Fassett Collective large prints in bright colorways.

## COMPOSITION

Another option is to continue the narrative from the collage to the background. Sometimes, animals need to be in an outdoor setting. You can create a layered landscape for the background using various textured fabrics. However, the collage can be placed into a simple landscape that is just a line to indicate the ground or floor. The key here is to make the landscape not overwhelm the collage.

These dogs were both outside, so it is natural to place them on grass with the sky around them.

## COLLAGED OR CURATED

These black-and-white curated fabrics make the perfect background for this brightly colored cow quilt.

This background choice is a way to combine multiple fabrics to create one background. You still use raw-edge fabrics and glue. To create this kind of background you need to:

**1.** Figure out the approximate size of your finished quilt, then cut backing and batting slightly larger. Layer these and position the collage on top. The goal now is to cover the batting with small pieces of fabric.

**2.** Choose a color scheme, either neutral, black and white, or a complementary or contrasting color to your collage. Your palette can be brightly colored or low volume. This is a good opportunity to incorporate fussy cut designs, so keep that in mind as you search for your fabrics.

**3.** Free-cut round-off shapes or designs, aiming to let fabrics blend into one another. Make sure the fabrics tuck under your collage. Layer and glue down your collage. Press. This is a good technique for using up small scraps.

## PIECED

If you enjoy piecing and want to spend the time putting together a pieced background, this is a great option. I caution you to carefully select your fabrics and colors to ensure they don't overwhelm the collage. Using a contrast-color family or neutrals would work.

## IMPROV PIECED

My favorite kind of piecing to do is improv style. Think of a crazy quilt where scraps or small pieces of fabric are joined to make a larger, usable piece of fabric. Just as with pieced backgrounds, make sure you carefully choose your fabrics and colors. This is a good option if you have fancy fabrics like lace or table linens that read as neutral but have an interesting texture.

When a background is improv pieced, the shapes and angles can easily blend into one another while still looking unique.

## PRINTS ON FABRIC SHEETS

I enjoy creating fabrics by printing "stuff" on fabric sheets. The options are endless. Think about laying items like leaves, buttons, food wrappers, etc. on the scanner bed of your printer and printing onto fabric. Consider handwriting or letters. I used school papers my son was throwing away. Handwritten music is personal and can follow a music theme. Available online are downloadable "junk journal" sheets for paper collage. Try printing them on fabric, but remember they will only be 8½" x 11" (21.6 x 27.9cm). Search for vintage ephemera, junk journals, collage sheets, botanicals, printable collage pages, etc.

## HAND PAINTED OR SURFACE DESIGN

If you love dyeing or painting fabric, playing with monoprinting, stamping, etc., you can make your own fabric for a background. All these types of fabric are totally unique. When I started quilting, I did not have a lot of money to spend on fabric; I would buy inexpensive muslin, then paint and dye it.

## BORDER OR NO BORDER

I often forget there is the option to add a border to collaged quilts. However, adding a border using print fabric related to your collage could be a good way to elevate your theme. Borders will also increase the size of the quilt and can act as picture frames. Add the border once the collage is glued to the background.

# Attaching the Background

The final step is to glue the collage to the background fabric. All you need is a little glue around the edge of the collage. You can also just pin your collage to the background. I do this if I want to stitch my background first. Having it pinned means I can stitch behind the collage to change direction as the stitches will be hidden. This is covered more in the next section, Free-Motion Quilting for Collage.

Congratulations! Your quilt top is made. I like to hang mine on a design wall so I can see it as it would be viewed rather than seeing it on the worktable. Step back and take photos. You might notice areas or pieces to change or alter. If needed, cut a new piece and just glue it on.

Create your own fabric prints by using items, papers, or free materials online. These can add something special and personalized to any project.

I added a border to look like a picture frame, which can elevate any wall hanging to fit into other important photos on the wall.

# Free-Motion Quilting for Collage

Free-motion quilting on collage is very forgiving, so have fun, relax, and just "go for it!" Children love to free-motion stitch as they have a worry-free approach. By lowering the feed-dogs and having the correct foot on, your sewing machine can go from stitching straight lines to sewing in any direction, even backward! If you are a novice, I suggest starting with a quilt sandwich (three layers of a quilt: quilt top, batting, backing) to get the feel of moving and stitching in all directions. To practice, you can draw lines on paper showing how you plan to stitch, which will help you visually and attune your brain!

## Getting Started

I will describe how I approach free-motion quilting to give you the essentials for your own projects.

These two free-motion feet, a closed or open-toe, work in the same way. The open-toe allows you to see the collage underneath more easily.

### PREPARING TO SEW
I stitch on a JUKI TL-2010Q, which is a semi-industrial, purely straight stitch machine. It is a work horse! I lower the feed-dogs, change to a darning or embroidery foot, set my stitch length to zero, and reduce the pressure on the presser foot. The setup of every sewing machine will be different, so refer to your manual if you are unsure.

### PREPARING YOUR QUILT TOP
Begin by preparing the three layers of the quilt. You have completed your quilt top by attaching your collage to the background fabric; the remaining layers are the batting and backing. Using your pressing table, lay the backing fabric wrong side up and press. Layer the batting onto this. Then center the quilt top right side up. Press. The backing and batting should be a few inches larger around the length and width than your quilt top. Baste or hold together the layers; I use just a few safety pins.

## DENSITY OF STITCHING AND THREAD PAINTING

Stitching can add an extra element to your quilt, but it's good to know if you want to show a lot or a little before starting.

The more experience I gain with free-motion quilting, the more stitching I add to my quilts. When starting out, work at the density you are most comfortable with. Thread painting is a term for quilts that are almost, or totally, covered by stitching. The fabrics can be obscured and all you see is the thread. For my collage projects, I don't like to cover all my fabrics. My goal is to secure the fabrics (as the glue is only a temporary hold) with the stitching, which adds texture and character to the surface.

### THREAD TAILS

Dealing with thread tails can be a chore depending on the finish of quilt you desire. Visually, my quilts contain a lot of stitches, textures, patterns, and raw edges, so I am not afraid to trim my threads. Some quilters, especially for show quilts, will "bury their threads." This involves tying them off and threading them individually into the quilt. I want to make quilts and not spend my time doing this! If you are happy to bury threads, go ahead.

My method when starting to stitch is to bring the bobbin thread to the top, hold the threads, and stitch a couple of mini stitches in that spot. I finish stitching in the same way, then trim the thread tails.

## Tips for Stitching

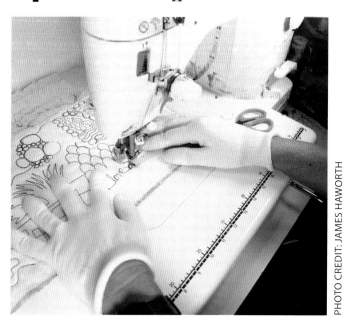

These gloves are lightweight, so I barely notice I'm wearing them once they're on.

- **I like to wear gloves** when I free-motion quilt, although it is easy to forget to put them on. The advantage is that they grip the quilt and protect your hands from fatigue. My favorite kind are the Machingers® by Quilters Touch.

- When considering the stitch patterns to use, **think about your subject matter**. You could attempt to imitate nature. Some examples: for a sky, stitch horizontal lines or simple clouds; for trees and bark, sew woodgrain patterns; for grass, stitch vertical lines as blades of grass. Looking at a photo can help to find inspiration or act as a guide. When I have had quilts in quilt shows, the judges have liked to see stitch patterns that relate to the theme of the quilt.

- **Every piece of fabric needs to be stitched on in some way**. If I am stitching around a fabric piece, my stitch line will be as close to the edge as I can without falling off. With raw-edge fabric, you do not want to stitch right on the edge, as this would encourage more fraying.

- **Carefully stitch around the details for small pieces**. For eyes, I like to stitch around every circle, color matching the thread—even the highlight.

The zigzags across the ground of this quilt give the impression of blades of grass, which helps to convey the forest path design.

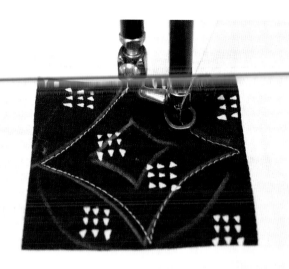

You can sketch straight lines or curves, which makes it easier to stitch patterns that are hard to eyeball.

- **Consider your thread color.** If you are new to free-motion quilting and are not confident in your results, choose a colored thread that will blend into your fabric choice. If you want your stitch patterns and skills to be on show, choose a contrasting-colored thread that will enhance and add to your theme.

- Straight stitch is the go-to stitch for free-motion, but you can also set your machine on a **zigzag stitch**. As you freely move your fabric stitching in zigzag, it will feel more erratic and produce great texture. Make sure to have the darning or free-motion foot attached or you will break the needle.

- It can be useful to **draw on the fabric using a chalk marker**. This will guide the direction of stitching, helping you keep lines straight and an equal distance apart. Painter's tape can also be a good tool to help when stitching straight lines.

- **Consider the dimensionality of your quilt.** Stitching densely will flatten an area and make it recede. Less stitching will make an area pop or come forward, giving a three-dimensional appearance.

- I usually **start near the center of the quilt** and work out, with the background being stitched last.

- **If using the same thread in another area**, instead of cutting your threads between each piece, lift the presser foot and move your fabric to the spot to be stitched. The rule is to stitch in the same spot, called a stay stitch, at the start and end of stitching. Clip your threads if they are in the way or tidy up later. Remember, you will have to trim the threads on the back also!

- **Free-motion quilting on a large quilt** is more challenging, but can be done on your home machine. It is useful to support the quilt on chairs or tables around your sewing area so the quilt is not dragging and causing it to pull at the machine.

# Making Original Stitch Patterns

Starting to stitch on your quilts is a daunting process. If you feel this way, let me say: you are not alone. I have been free-motion quilting for nearly twenty years and still feel trepidation when the collage is done and the quilt is ready to stitch. But without wanting to discourage you, once I start the process and the quilting is getting done, I am hooked and keep going until it is finished.

My first piece of advice is to look at your design as different areas—break it up. Then think about the various textures or patterns you want to portray (i.e., long fur on an animal, texture of a nose, bark of a tree, the smooth texture of wood, or the feeling of water). Each area will be stitched in a different pattern using a different colored thread. Free-motion quilting is a way to flatten and fill in the background in an even manner using a continuous line, as much as possible. You might want to draw these patterns or designs on a piece of paper just to familiarize yourself with how you would do this as a continuous line when using your sewing machine.

Looking at my sampler, I will describe what I was thinking about. At the top, I stitched horizontal wavy lines that represent the sky, even creating small cloud shapes and echoing these with more stitching. If I was to stitch on green fabric (representing a grass area), I would stitch rows of small grass sprigs, repeating them in horizontal lines. Or with my stitching, I could draw small plants with leaves and flowers for the grass. These quilting designs might

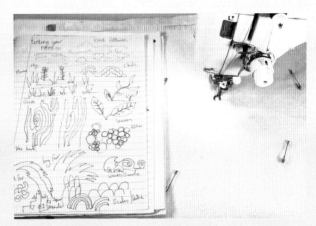

Before I made a stitch sampler I drew the kinds of stitch patterns, almost like a rehearsal.

be subtle, but on closer inspection, they do relate to what they are portraying. When stitching an animal, looking at a photo may help you decide on a texture to stitch, like long or short fur, feathers, scales, or spots. I do like to stitch around the fabric pieces I have collaged and include them in the stitching design. Other patterns to stitch include: small circles in various sizes used for rocks or skin texture, wood grain on trees, or wavy lines for water.

I hope these ideas help to quell that initial trepidation when starting to stitch a project. First, stitch the areas that you have planned and are more confident about. Moving around the quilt should not be a problem. Then gradually fill it all in. If you get stuck, look at photos for inspiration. Practice either by drawing the design or stitching on a practice quilt. Jump in and start quilting. You've got this!

This sampler shows a variety of patterns used to give texture or as a filler. I used a dark thread on a white fabric layered with batting and backing fabric.

Your stitch designs can match your theme in other ways, such as adding fur texture to an animal.

# When to Stitch the Background First?

As mentioned before, when choosing a background, I like to glue the finished collage onto the background and then stitch. In some cases, I will attach the collage to the background with pins so I can stitch the background first. I use this approach when a stitch pattern on the background fabric continues behind the collage. This enables me to stitch the background and easily move to another spot without worrying about the collage on top. When done, the travel stitching can then be hidden behind the collage.

Sometimes knowing what pattern to stitch, especially in the background, can be daunting. I look at quilting books or online for quilt pattern ideas. It also helps to consider the theme. I hope these tips have helped you, and that you are excited to finish your project. I enjoy the extra layer of interest and texture that free-motion stitching brings to the quilt. Just relax and have fun.

This fence wire pattern behind the dog is a good example of when you would stitch the background first, with the dog pinned to the quilt.

For this small grid background, I stitched the whole background first and then applied my collage.

# Finishing Your Project

Your collaged quilt is stitched, now what? For me, there are five different techniques to finish my collage quilts: a pillowcase finish, binding, facing, wrapping onto an art canvas, or a stitched edge. First, however, you need to trim your piece so it's the proper size and shape.

## Square Up the Quilt

For the first step, the quilt needs to be "squared up" and the excess fabric and batting trimmed away.

### Tips for Quilt Sizing

- **When adding a binding**, the quilt size will finish at the same size you cut it.

- **If you are adding a facing**, add ¾" (2cm) to the width and length for the finished size required.

- **For the pillowcase method**, use ½" (1.3cm) seam allowance and add 1" (2.5cm) to your cut size.

- **For a canvas frame**, you need to measure the depth of the frame to calculate your final cut size.

**1. Make sure you have square corners.** Use a large square ruler and line the ruler over your corner, keeping any horizontal design details parallel to the edge of the quilt. Cut with a rotary cutter.

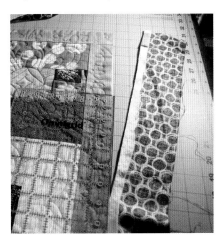

**2. Continue to trim down the side of the quilt using a longer ruler.** Turn the quilt, then repeat on each corner and side. If you need a certain size for the finished quilt, this is where you would measure and cut to size.

# Pillowcase Technique or Envelope Finish

This technique is good to use on smaller or more simple items like placemats or wall hangings. It keeps the edges flat, and no extra fabric is needed. **This method is done before the quilting, so you need to think ahead.**

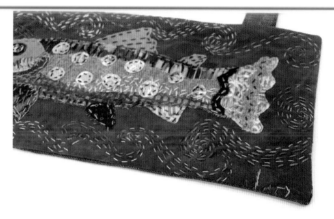

**1.** Place the quilt top right sides together onto the backing fabric with batting underneath. Stitch around using a ½" (1.3cm) seam, remembering to leave an opening.

**2.** Turn the quilt right side out through the opening. Press and hand stitch the opening closed.

Alternately, you could layer your quilt with batting, do your quilting first, then join as above. This means all the stitching is hidden within the quilt and no stitching will show on the back of the quilt.

# Covered-Zipper Pillow Back

There are any number of ways to finish a pillow back. I prefer a covered zipper treatment for attractiveness and ease in inserting a pillow form. This example is for a 20" (50.8cm) square pillow. Note: Contrast color zipper used for visual purposes. Remember to cut your back pieces and cover strip 1" (2.5cm) wider than the finished size of your pillow to accommodate a ½" (1.2cm) seam allowance.

### SUPPLIES
- Two 12" x 21" (30.5 x 53.3cm) fabric pieces for back
- Two 4" x 2" (10.2 x 5.1cm) fabric pieces for tab
- 3" x 21" (7.6 x 53.3cm) fabric strip for zipper cover
- 20" (50.8cm) all-purpose zipper
- Quilting ruler
- Rotary cutter and cutting mat
- Sewing machine and supplies (page 13)

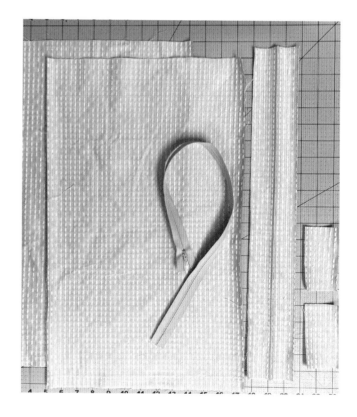

## INSTRUCTIONS

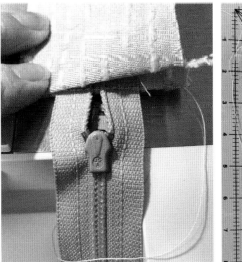

**1.** **Determine the top of the zipper.** Center and pin the top zipper ends, right sides together, to one 2" (5.1cm) side of a tab piece. Stitch with a ¼" (6.4mm) seam allowance.

**2.** **Turn under the opposite 2"** (5.1cm) **end of the attached tab** ¼" (6.4mm). Finger press. Fold the tab over, aligning the folded edges as shown over the end of the zipper. Pin if needed, and edge stitch through all layers. Lay out the zipper with the finished end along the 21" (53.3cm) edge of one pillow back piece.

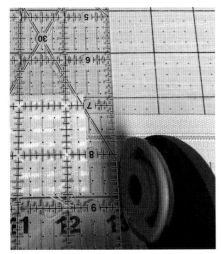

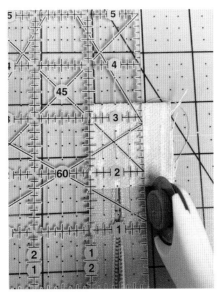

**3.** **Mark the end of the zipper 1½"** (3.8cm) **in from the opposite side of the pillow back piece.** Position your second pillow tab ¼" (6.4mm) beyond that mark, right sides together. Stitch using a ¼" (6.4mm) seam allowance (this is the same process as for the top of the zipper). Your stitching should align with the marking. Trim off the excess zipper, leaving no more than ½" (1.2cm). Fold over and finish as for your previous tab.

**4.** **Trim the tab on each zipper end in line with the zipper tape.**

**5.** **Fold the zipper cover in half wrong sides together lengthwise.** Press. Pin to the bottom 21" (53.3cm) edge of the one pillow back piece. Baste with a ¼" (6.4mm) seam allowance.

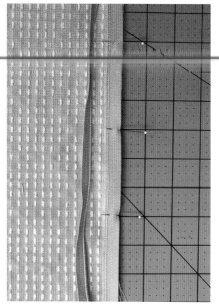

**6. Unzip the prepared zipper.** Pin wrong sides together (left side of the zipper as shown) to the 21" (53.3cm) top of the remaining pillow back piece. The opposite side of your zipper will be unattached and to the right of the pillow edge.

**7. Use a zipper foot.** Stitch the zipper to the pillow back using a ¼" (6.4mm) seam allowance. As you approach the zipper pull, leave the needle down, zip the zipper closed, and then continue stitching to the end.

**8. Press the pillow back piece along the zipper tape.** Edge stitch. Close the zipper.

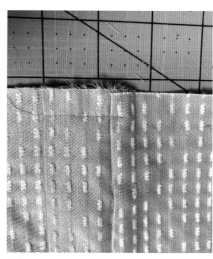

**9. Right sides together, place the remaining pillow back piece with cover strip attached.** Align it with the unattached edge of the zipper tape as shown. Pin and stitch, using a zipper foot and ¼" (6.4mm) seam allowance.

**10. On right side, stitch down the cover strip at the sides.** Use a ¼"–½" (0.6–1.2cm) seam allowance. Your pillow back is complete. Trim to 21" (53.3cm), join right sides together to pillow front, and insert form through zipper opening.

# Stitched Edge

This method is to add a border of dense stitching to finish the edge of the quilt. The flat edge will show raw edges and serendipitous stitching. Try this technique if you are happy with a casual, natural finish and not a precise edge. I encourage you to play around and have fun!

In this example, I made a border using squares of fabric that I stitched down using black thread. I added dense stitching around the outside of the quilt using circles and scribbles. I trimmed the edge of the shell quilt, but a white line of batting was visible, so I painted it with black acrylic paint.

# Facing

I use a facing when there are a variety of elements or fabrics in the background. The facing wraps all the way to the back of the quilt so no fabric shows on the front. The facing is ideal for pictorial or art quilts. These are the basic steps for how to add a facing, but more detailed tutorials can be found online.

**1. Cut four strips of fabric, 2¼" (5.7cm) x WOF.** Two need to be 2" (5.1cm) shorter and two 2" (5.1cm) longer than the sides of the quilt. Join extra strips as needed. Press a ¼" (6mm) fold to the wrong side along all the strips. Attach the shorter strips to the vertical sides of the quilt. Use a ¼" (6mm) seam allowance. Place 1" (2.5cm) down from the top edge, and finish with 1" (2.5cm) away from the end. Pin the longer strips to the horizontal sides, laying the extra 1" (2.5cm) over each end.

**2. Start stitching ¼" (6mm) from the corner on the longer pieces.** Then back stitch. Finish sewing at ¼" (6mm) from the end of the quilt and backstitch. Cut away a ¼" (6mm) square in each corner. You are removing bulk. Press the strips away from the front of the quilt. Topstitch a row ⅛" (3.2mm) away from the pressed seam to hold the strips open.

**3. Place on your pressing table with the back of the quilt facing you.** Fold the facing to the quilt so the quilt edges are even. Press and pin as you go. Use the longer strips to fold a neat, square corner. Cut away any extra fabric and pin. Hand stitch to finish.

# Wrapping a Canvas Frame

I like the immediacy of finishing my quilt this way, especially if it is a gift. I don't need to worry about a backing fabric or adding any kind of binding or facing. Be sure to measure the depth of the frame; it is important to make your quilt large enough that it can be wrapped and stapled to the back of the frame. Alternatively, make the quilt the same size as the canvas, then add fabric borders that wrap around the frame. To finish, add a wire or picture hanger and write your label on the back.

**1. Calculate the size you need to trim your quilt.** For a ¾" (2cm) deep frame, I include 1½" (3.8cm) on each side to be wrapped around. With the wrong side of the quilt facing up, center the canvas frame on the quilt. Working on two opposite sides, fold the quilt in and staple three times, avoiding the corners. Keep the quilt stretched and tight as you staple.

**2. Repeat on the remaining sides.**

**3. Trim away any excess batting and fabric from the corners.** Fold into a neat square, tucking in extra fabric. Staple in place. Add a picture frame wire for hanging. Write your label details on the back of the canvas with a permanent marker.

# Binding

A binding is a separate piece of fabric that finishes the edges and frames the quilt. For collage quilts, I use this method if the background is made of only one or two fabrics. This means I don't need to match my binding fabric color many times. My binding color choice is either the same fabric, one that blends, or one that highlights the collage. These are the basic steps for how I add a binding, but more detailed tutorials can be found online.

**1. Cut four strips of fabric.** Each strip should be 2¼" (5.7cm) wide; the length is the distance to fit around one edge of the quilt. Add 8" (20.3cm) to the approximate total binding length. Join the strips on the diagonal. Press the whole strip in half lengthways.

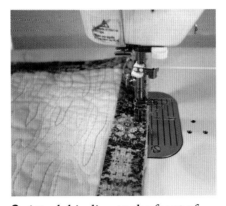

**2. Attach binding to the front of the quilt with a ¼" (6mm) seam.** Miter or fold the corners as you go. When you reach 8" (20.3cm) from the start of the binding, then measure, trim, and join with a diagonal seam. Attach to quilt.

**3. Fold the binding to the back of the quilt.** To finish, machine stitch from the front by stitching in the ditch or hand stitching.

## Other Finishing Touches

Finishing a quilt is more than deciding on a border or the medium it will be displayed as. Will it be a gift? What would personalize the piece? These questions are important to think about before you declare your work complete.

### SIGN YOUR QUILT

I always like to sign my quilts, as any painter would do on their artwork. When I finish a quilt, I free-motion stitch my signature "Jane H" into the lower-right corner. If you feel confident in your quilting skills, give this a try! It is fun to try to write using your sewing machine and thread!

### LABEL

Always add a label to your quilt! The label is a reference to when the quilt was made and by whom. This is especially helpful if you are giving a quilt as a gift. I add the name or title I have given the quilt, a short description, my name, the date it was made, where I live, and contact info like my website. To make my labels, I type them into the word processing application on my computer and print them on a fabric sheet. You can

I like to sign my name when I finish a piece, but you can also add someone else's name when it's a gift.

also handwrite your label using a permanent marker. I border the label by stitching it onto a colored fabric. Press in the edges and hand stitch onto the back of the quilt.

### WALL HANGING HARDWARE

Finally, add a hanging method of your choice. Traditionally a hanging sleeve is added to quilts, but an easier method of hanging wall quilts is to stitch on two small plastic rings. These hang onto picture hooks on the wall. Step back and enjoy your quilt, or gift it to a friend and make another.

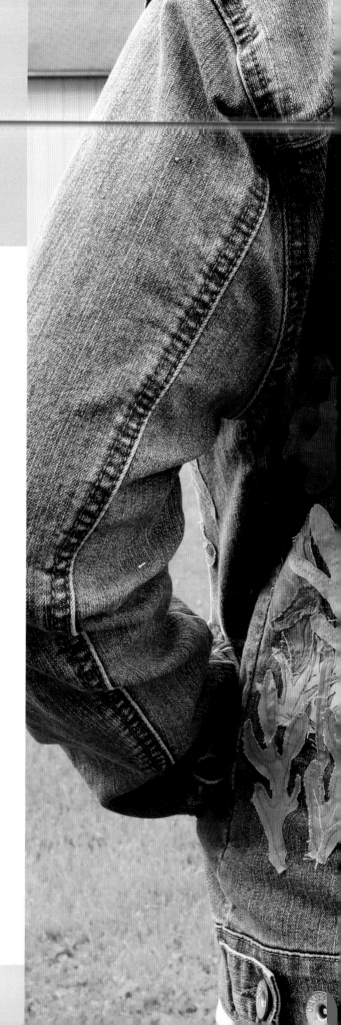

# chapter 3

# Projects

Now that you have learned to collage, and perhaps you have given collage a try, try your hand at one of the 12 projects included in this book. With some, I have included the pattern that you will need to enlarge as instructed. Or use the patterns at any size you desire, in a project like mine, or something totally different. Other projects are meant as a stepping stone or guide, so you can use the instructions and make a quilt or quilted project using your own ideas, photographs, and inspirations.

As you work through the projects, make sure you reference the skills and techniques explained in previous chapters. Not every step goes into full detail, so it's best to check as you get used to this new medium.

I have included a variety of themes that relate to my life that might inspire you to make your own unique quilt. A big part of my life has been traveling, visiting the ocean, and enjoying birds, landscapes, music, and pets. Think about a vacation you have taken and ways to capture those memories. Or a special pet's face that you wish to memorialize in a portrait quilt to hang in your home. Maybe you have always wanted to make a quilt of a childhood home to preserve those memories of living there.

Let *Capture Your Own Life with Collage Quilting* inspire you to take risks, design your own personal quilt projects, and let collage quilting become part of your life.

# Simple Layered Landscapes

**FINISHED SIZE: 12" X 12"** (30.5 X 30.5CM)

I have taken a ton of inspirational landscape photos on family trips and vacations, which includes lakes, coasts, seascapes, forests, mountains, meadows, fields, and sunsets. Any or all of these could be used as quilt designs. Simple, layered landscapes are impressionistic, and not a lot of fussy detail is needed. This project is different than the Heart and Home project (page 100), which includes more precise detail.

Some ideas to think about when planning a landscape quilt: Will this be a horizontal or vertical quilt? Can I use the rule of thirds when placing my horizon line? Is there an element I can use in the foreground to help create more depth in the scene? Do I have printed fabrics that will do the work for me? Can I fussy cut details like leaves, pinecones, etc. out of fabric? Finally, do I need to paint the sky to create the right atmosphere?

It can be hard to find a blue fabric suitable for a sky, and my solution is to paint it! This can be very helpful if you require a gray stormy sky, brilliant sunny sky, or sunrise or sunset. I will describe how I paint fabric for skies in these instructions.

For this first collage project, I want to keep things simple. I picked from four landscape images and mounted one on a canvas frame. The pattern is traced directly from the 8" x 10" (20.3 x 25.4cm) photo. I chose to use printed fabrics with patterns and textures that relate to the landscape theme. This project can easily be made as a 12" (30.5cm) wall hanging.

## SUPPLIES
- 8" x 10" (20.3 x 25.4cm) landscape photo in color
- Vellum or copy paper
- Black permanent marker
- Light box (optional)
- 13" x 13" (33 x 33cm) interfacing or stabilizer for foundation
- 13" x 6" (33 x 15.2cm) and smaller fabric scraps or off-cuts: assorted colors (greens, beiges, browns, etc.) to match landscape
- 13" x 13" (33 x33cm) cotton batting
- 12½" x 12½" (31.8 x 31.8cm) square quilting ruler
- Rotary cutter and cutting mat
- Two 2" x 40" (5.1 x 101.6cm) black fabric strips for a border
- 12" x 12" (30.5 x 30.5cm) art canvas
- Staple gun
- Collage supplies (page 13)
- Sewing machine and supplies (page 13)

## FABRIC PAINTING SUPPLIES
- 13" x 8" (33 x 20.3cm) white or cream fabric, washed and ready to paint
- Fabric for testing colors
- Acrylic or fabric paints in blue, white, black, pink, yellow
- Large flat paintbrush
- Water container
- Palette or plate for mixing colors
- Plastic table covering

# Painting the Sky Fabric

**1. Lay the fabric piece over a plastic table covering.** Pour paints into your palette. Add water to the colors to dilute, making it easier to blend with other paints. Spray or dampen your fabric with clean water; this will help the paints to soak in and bleed. Working in one area at a time, apply your paints using horizontal brush strokes.

**2. Quickly blend with other colors using more paint and more water.** Use the photo as reference for colors, texture, and mood. Have fun and be creative. The colors will appear lighter when they dry. Set your fabric aside to dry.

## Tip

Test your colors on a spare piece of fabric first. Dab small amounts of paint onto your palette. Experiment with blending colors, mixing with black and white paints, and diluting them. When confident with the colors, mix larger quantities in your palette.

# Making the Collage

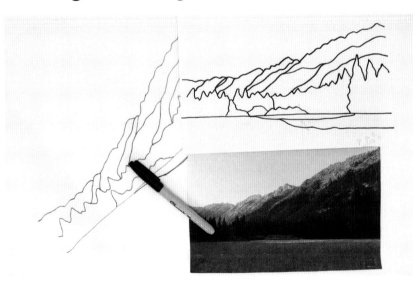

## Tip

Keep this design simple. If you have detailed lines on the design, smooth them out to make them less complicated as you trace them.

**3. Lay tracing paper over the photo.** Using a window or light box, trace the main details of the landscape. The 12" (30.5cm) quilt will be larger than the original photo or drawing, so you need to extend the design. Increase the sky or foreground area and extend the details on the sides. Place your foundation over the line drawing and transfer the lines to the foundation, extending where needed.

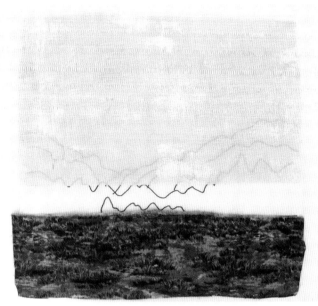

**4. Cut foreground details like trees and bushes, then set aside.** Since the sky and foreground are the largest areas, cut these pieces next. Make them large enough so the layers can overlap other areas where needed.

**5. Cut layers, but set them aside if they obscure adjacent ones.** When cutting horizontal details like mountains, fields, etc., make a whole strip the width of the collage. Use darker fabrics in the foreground and lighter fabrics in the distance to create perspective.

**6. Finish cutting all your pieces out.** Reassemble the layers on the foundation. Work from the back of the landscape to the front.

**7. Place foreground elements like trees over top.** Details like plants, leaves, fences, etc. are the last pieces to assemble. More details can be added with stitching, so let the fabric do the work for you where possible. When your collage is complete, layer onto batting and press. Make sure everything is glued and ready for free-motion stitching (page 52). Stitch as desired. I quilted a cloud pattern into the sky.

# Mounting on a Canvas Frame

**8.** Trim your quilt to 12½" x 12½" (31.8 x 31.8cm). I used my square 12½" (31.8cm) ruler. Make sure your horizon line is level.

**9. Cut the black fabric strips.** Cut two strips measuring 12½" (31.8cm) and two more measuring 15½" (39.6cm). These will be used as a border around the outer edge of the canvas.

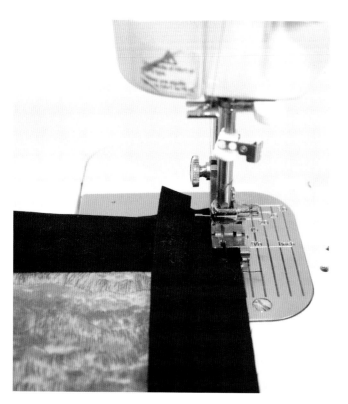

## Finish as a Wall Hanging

It's very simple to turn this quilt into a wall hanging. When the collage is complete, add borders (if required). Layer with batting and a backing fabric. Press. After quilting, trim to size. Add a binding, a label, and hanging sleeve or rings.

**10. Attach strips to the quilt using a ¼" (6mm) seam.** Stitch shorter pieces on the horizontal sides, press open, and add the longer pieces on the remaining sides. Press this seam open and press a ½" (1.3cm) seam all the way around to the back of the quilt.

**11. Apply a small bead of glue on the front edge of the canvas frame.** Like with the collage, glue is just to hold the canvas in place temporarily; the staples will be the permanent hold. Center canvas on the back of your quilt and press firmly.

**12. Wrap and staple quilt to the canvas.** See Wrapping a Canvas Frame (page 62) for more information. Now the quilt is complete and ready to hang! You can sign your artwork and write your label on the back of the canvas with a permanent marker.

# Bird on a Canvas Frame

**FINISHED SIZE: 14" X 11"** (35.6 X 27.9CM)

This small, quilted piece is made to attach to a stretched art canvas. These canvases can be purchased inexpensively at art and craft stores and come in a range of sizes. They make great gifts as they are compact and easy to hang.

For my composition, I used two collaged elements—the hummingbird and the fuchsia flowers—as well as some text. I like adding text to my quilts. I felt this project had space for a third element in the design. Find an inspirational word or phrase that you like. I purchased the artwork for the background as a downloadable "junk journal" paper design that I printed onto fabric sheets. There are many options for the background fabric design for this project. See my section Choosing a Background on page 47 for more ideas.

For this quilt, I did not enlarge the collage patterns for the hummingbird and flowers, instead using them at the original size. You are very welcome to make a bigger project and enlarge the patterns. You also have the option of making just the flowers or just the birds.

## Tip

You can use the same fabrics from the flowers for the hummingbird, which can add cohesion to the design.

## SUPPLIES

- Fuschia Flowers pattern (page 143)
- Hummingbird pattern (page 142)
- Vellum or parchment paper
- Collage supplies (page 13)
- Sewing machine and supplies (page 13)
- Liquid fabric stabilizer spray
- 14" x 11" (35.6 x 27.9cm) art canvas
- Quilting ruler
- Rotary cutter and cutting mat
- Staple gun
- Picture hanger

## FABRICS FOR THE FLOWERS

- Two 6" x 6" (15.2 x 15.2cm) pieces in different pinks
- Two 6" x 6" (15.2 x 15.2cm) pieces in different purples
- 4" x 4" (10.2 x 10.2cm) brown piece
- Three 6" x 6" (15.2 x 15.2cm) pieces in different dark greens

## FABRICS FOR THE HUMMINGBIRD

- 2" x 2" (5.1 x 5.1cm) white piece
- Three 4" x 4" (10.2 x 10.2cm) pieces in different grays
- Two 4" x 4" (10.2 x 10.2cm) pieces in different blacks
- Two 4" x 4" (10.2 x 10.2cm) pieces in different greens
- Two 3" x 3" (7.6 x 7.6cm) pieces in different pinks

## FABRICS FOR THE BACKGROUND

- Three 8½" x 11" (21.6 x 27.9cm) fabric sheets printed with downloadable artwork pieces
- Small pieces of neutral fabrics: enough to complete 18" x 15" (45.7 x 38.1cm) improv-pieced background
- 4" x 3" (10.2 x 7.6cm) fabric sheet printed with word "Inspire"
- 5" x 4" (12.7 x 10.2cm) green batik for word background
- 18" x 15" (45.7 x 38.1cm) cotton batting

# Making the Flowers

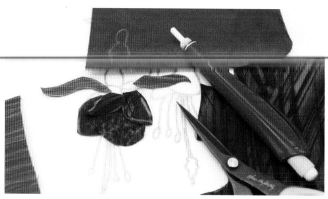

**1. Print out your pattern.** Attach a piece of vellum or parchment paper over it. This will prevent the glue in the collage from sticking to the paper pattern. For this small collage, I am not using any foundation. Lay flower fabric over the pattern and trace the shapes.

**2. Cut out the flower pieces.** If you feel confident, you can free-cut the shapes (page 37).

**3. Layer the flowers into single flower units.** Use small amounts of glue. The flowers don't need to be exactly the same because nature is rarely identical. The small stamen details will be made later with stitching.

**4. Cut out several leaf shapes in a variety of green fabrics.** Add narrow contrasting veins on some of the leaves. Cut stems using brown or dark pink fabrics.

**5. Build up the collage over the pattern.** Where the leaves overlap, add small amounts of glue to hold the different layers together. You should end up with three flowers and three leaf units. These will be combined fully when glued to the background. It's okay if your arrangement varies from my pattern. Remember, nature is eclectic.

## Tip

Use a stabilizer spray, such as Terial Magic, to stiffen your fabrics. This will make it easier to cut small details or pieces for your collage.

## Making the Hummingbird

**6. Use the larger hummingbird on the pattern sheet.** Print it out and cover with vellum or parchment paper. Use the instructions in Learning to Collage (page 32) for the construction of the bird. In that example, the hummingbird was enlarged at 225% and the pieces cut were larger. Keep this small bird simple. Details can be added later with stitching.

## Making the Word

**7. Type out your text on your computer.** Change the font and size to something you like. Print an example on paper and check how it fits on your collage. When satisfied, print on a fabric sheet.

**8. Trim a 1" (2.5cm) border around the word.** Along the edge, press a ¼" (6mm) seam allowance under to make a neat rectangle. Pin the word or phrase to the green batik fabric, leaving a 1" (2.5cm) contrast border around it. Stitch around to attach. Press a ¼" (6mm) allowance under the green fabric for a neat edge or leave as raw edge.

# Making the Background

**9.** Make your background so it measures 18" x 15" (45.7 x 38.1cm). There are various options here: a single piece of fabric, improv-pieced fabrics, or a painted piece of fabric. I joined four different fabrics to make my background. I suggest keeping the background neutral to let the collage stand out.

**10.** Layer the background fabric with the batting and press. Stitch or quilt the two layers together. I used a 1" (2.5cm) crosshatch pattern for my stitching.

## Border Option

The background fabric finishes at 18" x 15" (45.7 x 38.1cm), leaving a little extra to be trimmed down. However, to cover the 14" x 11" (35.6 x 27.9cm) art canvas, the background needs to finish at 17" x 14" (43.2 x 35.6cm). This allows for a 1½" (3.8cm) border or turning to wrap around the canvas on all sides.

# Assembling the Quilt

**11. Lay out your stitched background.** As you start placing the collage pieces, remember the 1½" (4cm) outside border that will be part of the wrapped canvas. Mark this using pins or chalk. Position your flowers, hummingbird, and word so they are within the marked frame. Leaves can flow over the top edge. Glue these pieces down.

**12. Stitch with free-motion stitching.** Change your thread colors to match or contrast. Stitch around the border of the word. Add details, such as stamens on the flowers, veins on the leaves, or feathers on the hummingbird.

# Mounting on a Canvas Frame

**13. Trim the piece down to 17" x 14"** (43.2 x 35.6cm). I used my cutting mat to measure and a quilting ruler to achieve straight lines.

**14. Apply a small bead of glue on the front edge of the canvas frame.** Center canvas on the back of your quilt and press firmly. Wrap and staple quilt to the canvas. Add a picture hanger to the back. You can sign your artwork and write your label on the back of the canvas with a permanent marker.

# Colorful Cat Pillow

**FINISHED SIZE: 20" X 20"** (50.8 X 50.8CM)

Not all collage quilts need to be made into wall decorations. For this project, I decided to make a large pillow cover. I chose to use a photo of a friend's cat, named Jade, who is incredibly fluffy. Although she is gray, I decided to give her the look of a ginger tabby using handmade batik fabrics from Turtle Hand Batik. These handmade batik fabrics are perfect for collage as they are slightly stiffened through the batik process, which means they fray less and are easier to cut. I included a range of values with pink, orange, and gray fabrics.

You may wish to use your own cat photo and pattern, or use the instructions below for making my cat pattern. Refer to the Guide to Making Animals and Pets (page 40) for more tips.

## SUPPLIES

- Pattern (page 144)
- 20" x 20" (50.8 x 50.8cm) interfacing or stabilizer for foundation
- Collage supplies (page 13)
- Sewing machine and supplies (page 13)
- 12wt white cotton thread
- 20" (50.8cm) zipper
- 22" (55.9cm) square pillow insert

## FABRICS

- Assorted fabric pieces in chosen color palette (I used grays, pinks, and oranges)
- Two 4" x 4" (10.2 x 10.2cm) fabric pieces in different colors for the eye
- 8" x 8" (20.3 x 20.3cm) black fabric
- 21" x 21" (53.3 x 53.3cm) fabric for the background
- 21" (53.3cm) x WOF for the pillow backing
- 22" x 22" (55.9 x 55.9cm) cotton batting
- 22" x 22" (55.9 x 55.9cm) muslin

# Making the Collage

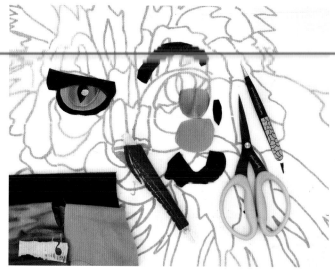

**1. Enlarge the pattern at 250%.** Trim and tape the pages together. Lay your foundation over the pattern. Attach with tape at the corners. Consider where you will use your different fabrics and colors. Roughly distribute your fabrics over the pattern and take a photo. Then remove.

**2. Trace and cut two fabrics for the iris and corners of the eye.** Layer them. When cutting these pieces, extend some extra fabric at the top of the eye; the eyelid will layer over this for a neat finish. Cut the pupil in black fabric. Trace and cut black echo or eyeliner for under the eye. Cut black eyeliner for the top eyelid, making larger as the eyebrow will layer over this.

**3. Cut all the pieces for both eyes, including the small highlight.** Layer, and when happy, glue the layers. Lightly attach or glue the center of the eyes to the foundation so they will not move but you have access to layer fabrics around them.

**4. Roughly lay out your fabrics.** Look at your photo for color and fabric placement. I decided to group the color families and keep them in specific areas. My design plan is orange for the left face and ear, pink on the right. I switched the colors below the eyes. I used the gray and black fabrics for the tabby stripes.

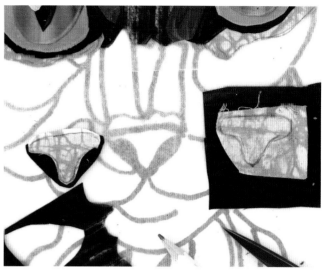

**5. Work on the focus areas first.** Add fabric around the eyes. Notice that I'm deviating slightly from the template, adding extra pieces in some places and simplifying in others. Let the fabric do the work when you can. There are no rules as to what to do or where to progress in collage.

**6. Make the nose.** Trace the nose shape onto a pink fabric, and cut it out. Hold the pink on black fabric, and cut an echo shape around it.

**7. Work above the eyebrows to the ears and top of head.** The top layer of fabric is what is closest to you (like the nose and eyebrows). Subsequent layers tuck behind those. When cutting fur, allow the points to be curved and smoothed. This will prevent fraying.

**8. Continue below the eyes.** Layers will tuck under as you work down. Use your fabric colors and values to create good contrast between the end of the chin and the body fur. Add glue between the layers as you work.

**9. Cut the pieces for the body.** These will be larger and less fussy. Have fun choosing fabrics and layering them.

**10. When you think you have finished your collage, take a photo.** Are there small, fussy-cut pieces you can add over larger fabric pieces? Add as desired. When happy with the result, glue everything down.

## Assembling the Quilt

**11. Cut away the excess foundation.** Preview the collage on various background fabrics. Look for good contrast. Position the cat on your background fabric and glue down.

**12. Layer the collage and background onto cotton batting and muslin.** Press. This is now ready for free-motion quilting. The threads I chose for the cat included a number of variegated threads in similar colors and plain, contrasting-color threads.

 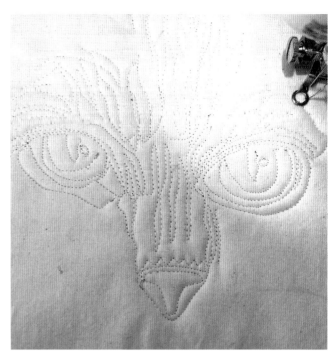

**13. Stitch the cat and the background.** Include fur patterns as you free-motion quilt the cat. I chose a geometric pattern for the background that wouldn't distract from the colorful cat, but mimics the triangle-like fur shapes. Draw the whiskers with chalk, and stitch either by hand or machine using a thicker 12wt thread by stitching up and back.

## Making the Pillow

**14. Construct your pillow.** Insert a zipper into the pillow backing (page 58). Turn pillow cover to the right side and insert your 22" (55.9cm) pillow form into your 20" (50.8cm) pillow cover.

# Wildflower Runner

**FINISHED SIZE: 18" X 38"** (45.7 X 96.5CM)

On the pattern I provided for this project, there are just a few flowers of each variety. To include more, as I did on my quilt, you will need to cut multiples. This table runner is made using four different wildflower designs, so I duplicated those flowers and intentionally altered their shapes and sizes to make it look more interesting. For example, you will need to cut the stalks longer and add more flowers and leaves when making your lupines.

You can use my flower designs or create your own designs using your favorite wildflowers as inspiration. My advice when cutting these small flowers is to keep the shapes simple and, if possible, let the colors and patterns in your fabrics do the work for you. We are going for a watercolor look here. The table runner can be made to whatever size you require.

In this project, I use mixed media in the background to enhance that watercolor look. You can use any of the art supplies I have listed here, but I encourage you just to use what you have at home. Experiment with your paints or watercolor pencils first to see what you feel comfortable with and what look you prefer. If you don't have the supplies and want to skip this step, you can do that also.

## SUPPLIES

- Pattern (page 145)
- Vellum or parchment paper
- Collage supplies (page 13)
- Liquid fabric stabilizer spray
- Sewing machine and supplies (page 13)

## FABRIC PAINTING SUPPLIES

- Watercolor pencils, fabric paints, or acrylic paints (I used Derwent Inktense Blocks)
- Large paint brush or 1" (2.5cm) foam brush
- Water container
- Paper towels
- Palette or plate for mixing colors
- Plastic table covering

## FABRICS

- 4"–8" (10.2–20.3cm) assorted fabrics in oranges, purples, greens, yellows, and blues
- 13½" x 26½" (34.3 x 67.3cm) white, neutral, or muslin cotton for the background
- Three 1½" (3.8cm) x WOF plain green strips for inner border
- Two 7½" x 13½" (19.1 x 34.3cm) floral fabrics for short outer border (I used Clothworks Painted Patchwork Digital Blooms in light cream)
- Two 3½" x 38½" (8.9 x 97.8cm) floral fabric for long outer border
- 20" x 40" (50.8 x 101.6cm) backing fabric
- 20" x 40" (50.8 x 101.6cm) batting
- Three 2¼" (5.7cm) x WOF strips for binding

# Painting the Background Fabric

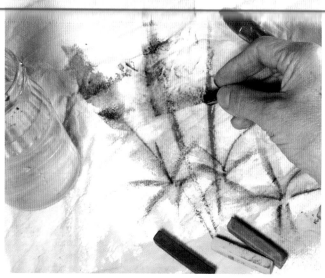

**1.** Lay the muslin or background fabric on a plastic table protector. Use a paintbrush or foam brush to paint water onto the background fabric to dampen it. Using your medium of choice, apply green color to form stalks and leaf shapes. Use your paintbrush dipped in water to blend and soften the marks. If using fabric or acrylic paints, water these down on the palette and apply in a gentle manner. Blend again using water on the cleaned paintbrush.

**2.** Apply appropriate colors to suggest flowers, leaves, and stems. These will be the base where your fabric flowers will be quilted, so plan your colors and shapes accordingly. Use plenty of water and blend using the paintbrush to create a watercolor look. Keep your marks simple for a muted appearance. Allow to dry, then heat-press.

# Making the Collage

## Tip

When cutting out my designs I use fabric stabilizer spray to stiffen my fabrics before cutting them. This product makes the fabric almost like paper and helps to prevent fraying. It isn't a necessity, but it does make cutting easier, especially when cutting out small shapes and using a free-cutting technique.

**3.** Cover your pattern with parchment paper to protect it from glue. Start with the poppies. Choose three values of orange fabric and begin tracing and cutting the petals. Work over the pattern lines, cutting the flowers and gluing them together. If making multiple poppies, you will need to extend the stalks and cut more leaf shapes in different sizes.

**Tip**

Cutting small flowers, leaves, and stems is organic. If you are confident, you can free-cut the shapes that you need. All flowers are different and they don't have to match my pattern precisely.

**4. Finish cutting and gluing the flower pieces together.** Transfer to the painted background. Arrange where the orange flowers are indicated on the fabric, and glue down. At this step, you may want to add more poppies; if so, cut extra stems, flowers, and leaves.

**5. Cut out the violets.** These include a white and yellow center, dark purple heart-shaped upper petal, and light purple lower petal. Cut and glue as you go. I made five flowers and several leaves. Transfer to the background fabric.

**6. Create the forget-me-nots.** Roughly cut the star-shaped flowers, and glue a turquoise circle in the center of each. Cut stems and leaves, then arrange on the background before adding the glue.

**7. Cut out the buttercups.** Trace, cut, and glue in a similar process to the forget-me-nots. These use dark yellow centers. Cut stems and then arrange on your background over the yellow painted area.

**8. Create the lupines.** Cut the stems and arrange on your background. Free-cut a number of jelly bean–shaped fabrics in a variety of purples, starting with light greens and lilacs at the top of the stalk. Arrange in loose rows and glue down. Cut a number of star-shaped leaves.

**9. Check for any open areas.** Don't be afraid to cut more leaves or grasses to give a balanced look across the collage. Make sure everything is properly glued down. Press.

# Assembling the Quilt   All seam allowances are ¼" (6mm).

**10.** Attach the inner border around all four sides. Press. Attach the two short slides of the outer border. Attach the two remaining borders on the length of the quilt. Press. Layer with the batting and backing fabric. Press the layers together and add safety pins approximately 8" (20.3cm) apart.

**11. Stitch around the fabric pieces.** Use threads in light and dark of the flower colors. Having a dark- and light-value color thread creates some contrast when stitching so the thread color stands out. Try stitching some shadow flowers in the background, especially if you have a section with no fabric collage over the painted background.

**12. Stitch up and down the stems and around the edges of the leaves.** Adding some leaf veins in a contrasting thread when you have room is a nice touch. For variety when stitching the leaves and stems, I used four different threads, including a variegated one. Add echo or shadow stitching in the background in any large painted areas.

## Tip

Instead of cutting your threads after stitching each piece, lift the presser foot. Move your fabric to the next area to be stitched, then stitch this piece. The rule is to stitch in the same spot, called a stay stitch, at the start and end of stitching one area. Clip your threads if they are in the way or when finished. Trim the threads on the back also.

**13. Change to straight stitch.** Stitch-in-the-ditch around both sides of the inner border, color-matching your thread so it doesn't show. Free-motion stitch in the outer border as desired.

**14. Trim the quilt to remove excess batting and backing fabric.** Finish the runner in your preferred method. Make and add a quilt label.

# Got the Blues

**FINISHED SIZE: 24" X 38"** (61 X 96.5CM)

This quilt was inspired by a friend's love of music. Whenever we visit, he will be playing his guitar and writing original music. I had to call this quilt "Norm's Guitar." The design started with a guitar photo, and I used music themed fabrics and large music notes to continue the idea. The background includes commercial-printed fabrics, copyright-free music sheets, and handwritten music printed onto fabric sheets. The musical notes are from the song "Somewhere Over the Rainbow."

When choosing the colors for the guitar, I wanted to keep with wood tones, but I exaggerated the values going from a dark brown through to gold. To contrast the brown tones of the guitar, I choose blue fabrics, including some prints for the guitar neck and pick guard.

## SUPPLIES

- Pattern (page 146)
- 22" x 30" (55.9 x 76.2cm) interfacing or stabilizer for foundation
- Collage supplies (page 13)
- Liquid fabric stabilizer spray
- Sewing machine and supplies (page 13)
- 12wt white cotton thread
- 12" x 12" (30.5 x 30.5cm) freezer paper

## FABRICS FOR THE GUITAR

- 10" x 12" (25.4 x 30.5cm) black fabric
- Eight 16" x 12" (40.6 x 30.5cm) assorted fabrics in brown through gold
- 10" x 16" (25.4 x 40.6cm) gold fabric for sound hole
- Three 10" x 6" (25.4 x 15.2cm) assorted fabrics in blue
- 10" x 10" (25.4 x 25.4cm) blue fabric for sound hole
- 6" x 18" (15.2 x 45.7cm) blue fabric for neck

## FABRICS FOR THE FOREGROUND AND BACKGROUND

- 22" x 12" (55.9 x 30.5cm) red fabric for the music notes
- Eight 10" x 12" (25.4 x 30.5cm) fabric pieces in assorted light colors for the background (I printed some on fabric sheets)
- 26" x 9" (66 x 22.9cm) dark or black fabric for the base
- Printable fabric sheets (optional)
- 28" (71.2cm) x WOF batting
- 28" (71.2cm) x WOF backing fabric
- Four 2¼" (5.7cm) x WOF black fabric strips for binding

# Making the Guitar

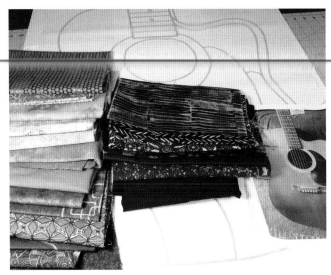

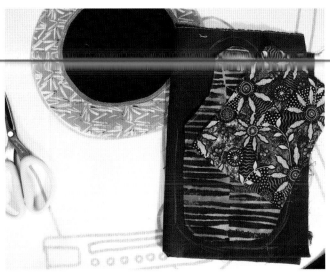

**1.** **Enlarge the pattern at 325%.** Trim and tape the pages together. Extend the neck of the guitar by 6" (15.2cm) so the guitar measures 19" x 31" (48.3 x 78.7cm). Cut a piece of foundation that will cover the guitar. Secure with painter's tape.

**2.** **Trace, cut, and layer three circles of fabric for the sound hole.** Start with a black circle, surround with a narrow circle of gold, and glue these together. Cut the largest circle in blue fabric and layer with the other circles on top. Glue. Set aside. Trace the main shape of the pick guard (to the right of the sound hole). Place this on a darker fabric and cut a ¼" (6mm) echo. Use a third fabric to trace or fussy cut the details. Glue these layers together. Set aside.

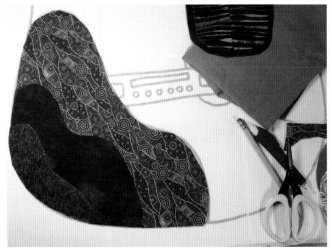

**3.** **Make the rectangular bridge.** Trace the shape and fussy cut the small details. I included a black strip of fabric that is the same size and shape of the blue print bridge. When placed underneath, it looks like this piece has dimension. Glue and set aside.

**4.** **Work on the guitar body.** Arrange your fabric choices from dark brown to a gold or light brown. Starting at the bottom left corner, trace and cut the first shape using the darkest fabric. Continue working up the guitar, tracing and cutting your shapes. Include a fabric allowance where a piece will tuck under the previous one. Glue these together and glue or attach to the foundation. Do not use too much glue.

**5. Progress up the guitar body.**
Arrange the circular sound hole, overlapping the guitar pieces. Position and glue in place. Position the pick guard and bridge. Glue in place over the guitar fabrics. You will need to look under the fabrics at the pattern to locate exact positioning of these pieces.

**6. Cut the neck of the guitar.**
Remember it is approximately 6" (15.2cm) longer than the pattern size. As with the bridge in step 3, add black fabric underneath for the illusion of dimension. Cut thin strips for the frets and cut circles for the fret markers. It's important for these pieces to have good contrast, especially when using a print for the neck. Position in place and glue.

**7. Press the collage.** Trim away all the excess foundation around the guitar.

## Making the Background

**8. Consider how the background area will be filled with improv piecing.** Begin by joining two small pieces of fabric and layering under the guitar. Trim down your next fabric and attach. As you work, return the background to the pattern so you always know approximately what shape and size piece of fabric is needed. Sew, press, attach another fabric, and trim as you go. Off-cuts can be attached elsewhere in the piece. Once you have covered the background, leave an allowance behind the guitar that will be covered when it is glued in place.

**9.** **Cut a long, dark fabric piece for the base of the quilt.** Press and fold under approximately ¼" (6mm) along the top edge. This will create a sharp edge. Position and glue to the bottom of the background.

**10.** **Lay the quilt background on a flat surface.** Position the guitar collage on top. Glue around the outside edge of the guitar, attaching it to the background. Press. Assemble quilt with the backing fabric, batting, and quilt top. Press together and baste with safety pins.

# Free-Motion Stitching

**11. Stitch the sound hole, bridge, and frets.** Starting at the base of the guitar, stitch the outline in a brown thread and echo quilt the three lower-left shapes. Fill in the guitar, echoing the curves of the other cut pieces. I changed my thread color from dark brown to a moss green to a cream going up the guitar. Stitch the background with a variegated black and white thread in a triangle meander pattern. Using a ruler and chalk pencil, mark the six strings. Stitch up and back with 12wt cotton thread.

## Making the Music Notes

**12. Treat the red fabric with fabric stabilizer spray.** This makes it fray less and easier to cut. Plan the size of the music staff and draw wavy lines onto freezer paper. Iron the freezer paper to your stiffened red fabric and cut out five wavy lines ¼" (6mm) wide. Draw 4" (10.2cm) tall music notes on the freezer paper. Iron these together and cut out.

**13. Arrange the staff and notes onto your quilt top.** Glue in place. Free-motion quilt around the edges using red thread. Trim the quilt. Finish as desired.

## Tip

On a music sheet, the five horizontal lines are called a staff or stave. Music notes rest on the lines or the spaces between to indicate a certain note.

# Under the Sea

**FINISHED SIZE: 26" X 38"** (66 X 96.5CM)

As a Pisces, I love the ocean, fish, snorkeling, and visiting Hawaii. When I first learned about fabric collage, I was still fairly new to quilting and was inspired by Susan Carlson and her collaged fish. I started by including one fish per wall hanging, but when I wanted to make a large quilt, I knew I would have to spend time making schools of fish! If you enjoy making fish, settle into the repetition and make a lot of them!

This quilt includes three Moorish Idol fish. (I love seeing these while snorkeling in Hawaii.) If you don't have all the same fabrics as me, go with what you have. The freedom in collage to use scraps and small pieces is liberating. For the background fabrics, again, they don't need to look exactly like mine. Find something for the water; it could be a plain blue, hand dye, ombre, etc. Look at photos of ocean floors with plants, rocks, or coral, and try to find patterned fabrics that work there. The variety in batik fabrics is perfect. Have fun layering fabrics at the bottom of the quilt, preview, and take photos as you go.

## SUPPLIES
- Pattern (page 147)
- 10" x 34" (25.4 x 86.4cm) interfacing or stabilizer for foundation
- Collage supplies (page 13)
- Sewing machine and supplies (page 13)
- Freezer paper

## FABRICS FOR THREE FISH
- 9" x 9" (22.9 x 22.9cm) white piece
- 5" x 6" (12.7 x 15.2cm) gray piece
- 6" x 6" (15.2 x 15.2cm) light yellow piece
- 6" x 6" (15.2 x 15.2cm) sunshine yellow piece
- 9" x 9" (22.9 x 22.9cm) black piece
- 9" x 9" (22.9 x 22.9cm) blue-and-black piece
- 3" x 3" (7.6 x 7.6cm) orange piece
- 5" x 5" (12.7 x 12.7cm) turquoise piece
- 5" x 5" (12.7 x 12.7cm) black-and-white piece for the fin

## FABRICS FOR THE BACKGROUND
- 28" x 36" (71.1 x 91.4cm) fabric for the water
- Assorted fabric pieces for rocks, coral, sand, and plants
- 28" x 40" (71.1 x 101.6cm) cotton batting
- 28" x 40" (71.1 x 101.6cm) backing fabric

# Making the Fish

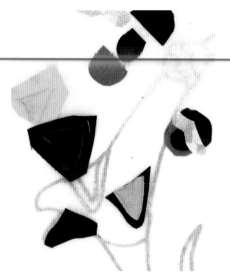

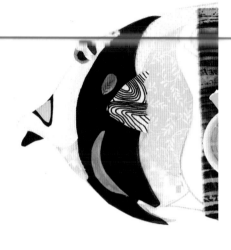

**1. Print fish pattern.** Cut a piece of foundation that will cover the fish. Secure with painter's tape. Starting on the left side, at the head, cut and layer the fabric pieces for the eye. Use blue, black, and gray fabrics. Glue and set aside. Cut, layer, and glue the black and yellow nose detail. Cut the black lower lip. Set these pieces aside.

**2. Trace and cut the side fin in the black-and-white fabric.** Set aside. Use the white and gray fabrics to make the head. Lay onto the foundation. Cut the black stripe and the orange dot detail.

**3. Continue to cut the layers, progressing to the right toward the tail.** Include an allowance on the left side of each piece as this will layer under the previous one. When happy, start to glue the layers in place. Secure with glue to the foundation. Locate where the side fin, eye, and other small details are positioned. Glue.

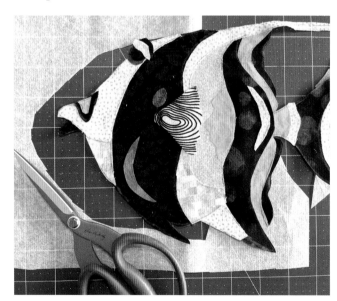

**4. When complete, make sure everything is glued.** Cut away the extra foundation. You now will have a completed fish.

**5. Make two more fish.** If you feel comfortable build two fish at the same time. The remaining two can be made together by layering the fabric, and cutting two at the same time. Remember all fish are not identical! You can vary the size and position to make them look unique.

# Creating the Background

**6. Lay down your water background on your worktable.** I like to use a single piece of fabric for the water and build layers of printed fabrics at the bottom to represent sand, rocks, corals, plants, and shells. Look for good contrast between fabrics. Arrange them before cutting to get a good sense of the layout, colors, and values.

**7. Start at the bottom and layer fabrics to represent sand, rocks, etc.** Start cutting or fussy cutting to create irregular shapes that look more natural. As you cut pieces, move them around and layer them from front to back. Just have fun here. Cut simple grass shape pieces with scissors or a rotary cutter.

**8. Create specific plants or corals.** Draw a simple design onto freezer paper, such as small black tree shapes. Iron the freezer paper to the front of the fabric, and cut out. Remember, you can reuse the paper templates.

# Stitching and Finishing

**9. Keep cutting and layering the fabrics.** Remember to create contrast. Arrange your three fish in natural-looking positions; they can even overlap each other. Take photos as you go. When you are happy with the design, glue everything down. Press.

**10. Layer the quilt top with batting and backing fabric.** Press. Free-motion quilt using a variety of colorful threads for your fish, including variegated threads.

**11. Match your stitch pattern to each area.** When stitching fish, I like to stitch a repeating scale pattern. If you are unsure, draw with chalk onto your fish and stitch over the drawn lines. For the background, stitch water-like patterns in wavy vertical lines. Keep stitching and changing colored threads until everything is stitched down. Trim to size. Finish as desired. Add a label on the back.

# Heart and Home

**FINISHED SIZE: 14" X 20"** (35.6 X 50.8CM)

A personal way to preserve the memories of a house you have lived in and loved is to make a quilt of that home. Perhaps it's the home of a friend or relative, a beautiful house in your neighborhood, or a striking building you have photographed. Imagine receiving a quilt of a new home or a home you were sad to leave behind. What great gifts these quilts could make. If you love the accomplishment of making this unique and personal quilt, perhaps take on the challenge of making a larger quilt combining homes in your neighborhood or town. The options for a Heart and Home quilt are endless. For this project, I chose to make a quilt of my house.

My techniques are to keep the collage simple (especially as I am working on a small size) and to find fabrics that will create the textures and patterns that I need for plants, grass, fences, roofing, siding, etc. I chose to stitch everything using a black thread to create pattern and texture. To make it personal, include clothing remnants or memory items from a family member. Try including some hand-stitched details as another layer of texture.

For this project, I will provide instructions on how I put *my* house quilt together. Adjust where it makes sense in your piece. I enlarged my photo by 150%, but don't be afraid to make a larger pattern, and thus, a larger quilt. Your fabric choices will also be your own, inspired by fabrics you already have and what you see in the photograph. Have fun finding fabrics, especially textured prints that can do the work for you.

## SUPPLIES
- 8" x 10" (20.3 x 25.4cm) house photo in color
- Vellum or copy paper
- Black permanent marker
- Interfacing or stabilizer for foundation
- Liquid fabric stabilizer spray
- Collage supplies (page 13)
- Sewing machine and supplies (page 13)
- 16" x 22" (40.6 x 55.9cm) cotton batting
- 16" x 22" (40.6 x 55.9cm) backing fabric
- Two 2¼" (5.7cm) x WOF strips for binding

## FABRICS
Measurements vary from 4" x 4" (10.2 x 10.2cm) to 16" x 6" (40.6 x 15.2cm)
- 3 different blues for pool water and sky
- 2 different pinks for decking and shadow
- Rock print fabric for waterfall
- 2 different grays for rocks and windows
- 5 different greens for trees and shrubs
- 2 different browns for dirt and roof line.
- White fabric for railings
- 2 different creams for siding
- Striped fabric for roof
- 2 prints for planters

# Making the Collage

## Tip

Remember to create contrast in your collage even if you must exaggerate what you see in the photo. It will make for a more successful collage. When working, keep the original color photo on your worktable as a guide for colors and fabric choices.

**1. Create the pattern.** Follow instructions in Five Methods of Enlargement (page 30) to draw your 150% enlarged pattern. Trace the pattern onto vellum or copy paper. Or use another method to print out and tape together.

**2. Gather your fabrics for the project.** Have fun finding those textured prints. Include different values so you can create shadows and highlights. Using fabrics printed with rocks, bricks, fences, trees, etc. can make those areas of your quilt look even closer to reality. Cover the pattern with the foundation and attach with painter's tape.

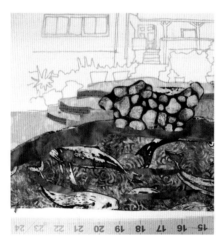

**3. Start your collage at a spot that feels like a focal point.** It could be a front door, a tree, or something else. I started with the pool water at the bottom of the photo and worked my way to the top. Fussy cut where appropriate, such as the rocks behind the waterfall.

**4. Build out your collage.** To create the steps on the pool deck, I used a pink hand-dyed fabric and a darker pink for the step shadow. Keep the shapes simple as too many small details will get confusing. For the planters, I used one fabric for the pot and one fabric for the plants; too much more will look overly fussy. Add glue as you make progress.

**5. Continue working up or away from your focal point.** Remember to include contrast between different textures and shapes. Cutting spiky green plants provides contrast to the gray rounded rocks. The line of soft green bushes will again provide contrast.

**6. Create the house or another important element.** Again, start with a focal point. I began with one section of the house that sticks out from the rest. Take advantage of your prints, such as using the dark line to replicate the shadow in this area. Before adding the sky, I included some softer tree areas using light and mid-green fabrics. They provide definition and contrast to the hard roof line.

**7. Work toward the more rigid parts of the house.** Because the porch railings are so small, I cut and added only a few. The rest will be stitched in. To make windows with a frame, cut the glass rectangle and then cut a slightly larger rectangle for the frame. Glue the two layers together, creating a small frame around the window. For the roof, I used a striped fabric to give the illusion of roof tile texture and solar panels.

**8. Add final details.** This can be flowers on the bushes, door handles, chimneys, etc. They can be free-cut and layered in place. Glue everything down.

## Stitching and Finishing

**9. Layer the completed collage with your batting and backing fabric.** Press. Add a few safety pins for basting. Free-motion quilt using a black 50wt thread. This finer thread will create pattern and texture when stitching rocks, tiles, striped siding, leaves, and flowers. Try to quilt evenly across the whole quilt. If you have a border, quilt a pattern here. Finish the quilt by adding a binding and label.

## Adding a Border

To finish this composition, you may leave as is or add a border. I decided to add a border to this house quilt of a small Hawaiian studio. I squared up the collage quilt top using a rotary cutter and ruler, cut a 3" (7.6cm) border, and attached it with a ¼" (6mm) seam. Press.

## Tip

To cut narrow or small details, like the ¼" (6mm) white railing on a porch, I treated my fabrics with stabilizer spray. It was easier and I felt more confident cutting narrow strips. Plus, the fabric will fray less.

# Upcycled Seashell Purse

**FINISHED SIZE: 16" X 12"** (40.6 X 30.5CM), **PLUS 9"** (22.9CM) **HANDLES**

Tote bags and purses demonstrate the versatility of collage. Instead of using the shell collages as a wall hanging, here I apply them to a purse, which is perfect as a gift for a friend. When possible, I like to use upcycled or repurposed fabrics in my work. This could include old clothing, bedding, linens, or vintage family textiles. In this project, I reused an old pair of jeans as well as many of my small fabric pieces and scraps. Repurposing scraps helps make this an environmentally friendly project.

To begin, I had a look at my seashell collection for inspiration. I'm sure you have one too! I painted the shells in watercolor, then drew them simply for a collage pattern. I came up with six different shell designs to include on this purse. For this project, I created the collage designs at the original size, but there is no reason why you couldn't enlarge the shells and use them in a wall hanging or as part of a seascape.

## SUPPLIES
- Pattern (page 148)
- Vellum or parchment paper
- Fabric collage supplies (page 13)
- Sewing machine and supplies (page 13)

## PURSE SUPPLIES
- Pair of old jeans, adult size
- ½ yard (45.7cm) fusible fleece or batting (I used Pellon FF78F1 Flex-Foam™)
- ½ yard (45.7cm) lining fabric (I used Treasure Island Jellyfish by Philip Jacob)
- 5" x 40" (12.7 x 101.6cm) blue fabric for side
- 3" x 40" (7.6 x 101.6cm) blue fabric for binding (same as side fabric)
- Two 3½" x 22" (8.9 x 55.9cm) denim strips for handles
- Two 1½" x 17" (3.8 x 43.2cm) fleece or batting strips for handle piping
- 1¼" x 6" (3.2 x 15.2cm) blue fabric for button loop
- Button or toggle for closure
- 2 snap fasteners

## FABRIC FOR THE SEASHELLS
Use scraps or small pieces approximately 6" x 6" (15.2 x 15.2cm)
- Small print fabrics in pink, cream, and peach:
  - 2 dark-value pieces in each color
  - 2 medium-value pieces in each color
  - 2 light-value pieces in each color

# Cutting

**1.** Cut both legs from the jeans at the crotch. Cut down the outside seam to open the legs. Cut and remove the bulky seam.

**2.** Cut one or both of the back pockets to include in the purse. Leave a ½" (1.3cm) border around the bulk of the pocket. You will use this to stitch on.

**3.** Select one jean leg. Cut two 16½" x 11½" (41.9 x 29.2cm) rectangles for your purse back and front.

**4.** Cut the bag side strip in denim or a contrast fabric. Make it 4½" x 38½" (11.4 x 97.8cm).

**5.** Cut the bag lining. You need two pieces at 20½" x 13½" (52.1 x 34.3cm).

# Making the Collage

**6.** Layer the parchment paper over the pattern and **attach with a little tape.** Make seven collaged seashells using the instructions in Learning to Collage (page 32). Start with the main body of each shell, then add fussy cut or free-cut details. Repeat one of the designs, making two of the same shell, for a total of seven shells.

**7. Attach front and back denim to the fusible fleece, or pin to batting.** Quilt these layers together as desired. Attach fleece or batting to the fabric side strip. Quilt.

**8. Arrange your shells onto the back and front pieces.** Six are lined on the front piece. Use the remaining shell in the bottom-right corner of the back piece. Keep the collage 1½" (3.8cm) from the outside edge. Free-motion stitch in place.

# Constructing the Bag All seam allowances are ½" (1.3cm).

**9. Attach the side gusset to the bag front.** Start at the top and stitch along three sides with a ½" (1.3cm) seam, turning at the corners. Attach to back in the same way. It's important to keep the bag top open to ensure the shells are not upside down. Turn to the right side.

**10. Attach the denim pocket to one bag lining piece.** Position it centered and 2" (5.1cm) down from the top edge. Stitch all the way around the jean pocket on the ½" (1.3cm) denim border.

**11. Make a fabric pocket.** Cut fabric to 6" x 8½" (15.2 x 21.6cm). Double fold one short side and topstitch. Press ½" (1.3cm) fold to the wrong side on three remaining sides. Topstitch pocket onto second lining piece along these sides, leaving the top open.

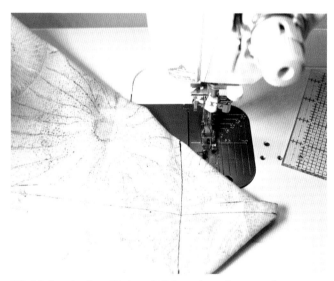

**12. Make the bag lining.** With right sides together, stitch around three sides of the lining, leaving the top open. Box the corners of the lining so it fits inside the bag. Center and flatten the bottom of the lining to form triangles. Square this off by stitching a 5" (12.7cm) seam on both sides. Trim off the excess fabric. Insert lining into main bag wrong sides together. Pin and stay stitch along top edge.

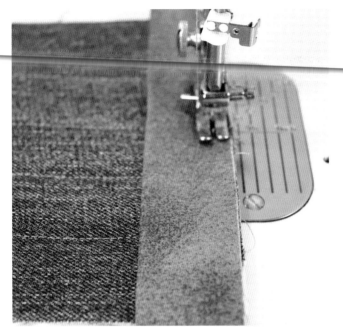

**13. Make a binding strip.** Press the 3" (7.6cm) strip in half. Attach binding along top edge of bag. Stitch binding to the right side of the bag. Join ends.

**14. Fold binding to the inside of the bag.** Pin or clip in place. Stitch from the front in the ditch, making sure to stitch through the binding underneath.

**15. Create handles.** To make handles, triple fold and stitch along the fleece or batting to make piping. Use denim from the second jean leg as your handle fabric. Insert the piping starting 2" (5.1cm) from the end of the handle fabric. Fold both edges to the inside as you topstitch to form a handle. Piping should end about 2" (5.1cm) from the end of the handle.

**16.** **Fold and press the handle ends in ½"** (1.3cm)**.** Flatten the end of the handle so it is ready to attach to the bag. You may need to unpick some of the seam.

**17.** **Pin handles to the bag about 4½"** (11.4cm) **from the side seams.** Keep the seam on the inside. Stitch a square in this flattened area. This can be tricky with the thickness of the bag and the denim.

**18.** **Attach a button and button loop for closure.** If desired, add snap fasteners on the top of the sides to create more shaping.

# Pet Portrait Quilts

**FINISHED SIZE: 24" X 32"** (61 X 81.3CM)

What could be more fun than making a quilt that brings back memories of a forever pet? This can be a challenge as you likely want this to be faultless and look just like your furry friend. But give yourself a break—ideally, you just need to catch that animal's spirit. As you make more collages, the technique will get easier and there will be less pressure on yourself to always make that "perfect quilt." Have fun!

In this book, there are various ways to use your pet photo in collage, such as a pillow, a wall hanging, or even a bed-size quilt. Here I will describe how I made this quilted wall hanging of Poppy, my cousin Amanda's childhood Saluki, but feel free to make yours at the size you want.

## SUPPLIES
- Pattern (create from your photo, page 41)
- 8" x 10" (20.3 x 25.4cm) animal photo in color
- 20" x 30" (50.8 x 76.2cm) interfacing or stabilizer for foundation
- Liquid fabric stabilizer spray
- Collage supplies (page 13)
- Sewing machine and supplies (page 13)

## FABRICS
- Two 4" x 4" (10.2 x 10.2cm) fabric colors for the eye
- Assorted fabric pieces in chosen color palette for the collage
- 8" x 8" (20.3 x 20.3cm) black fabric
- 25" x 33" (63.5 x 83.8cm) fabric for the background
- 26" x 34" (66 x 86.4) backing fabric
- 26" x 34" (66 x 86.4) cotton batting

# Making the Collage

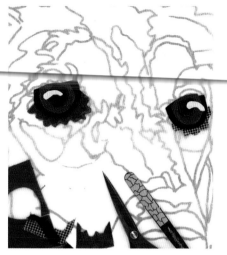

**1.** **Enlarge your pattern to 250%, print out, and tape together.**
Use painter's tape to secure the foundation over the pattern. For this quilt, I wanted to use the actual colors of the dog. The types of fabrics I included are mostly textures with small designs or prints on them. These include lines or stripes used to create the look of the long fur on the ears.

**2.** **Trace the parts of the eye.** Cut and layer the fabric pieces. For the eyes, I used rich brown, black, and white fabrics. When cutting small details, I treat the fabric with stabilizer spray to make them stiff.

**3.** **Construct both eyes.** Thanks to this angle, the eyes are almost identical in this piece. When you are happy, add your glue. Add glue behind the center of the eye to attach it to the foundation in its correct position.

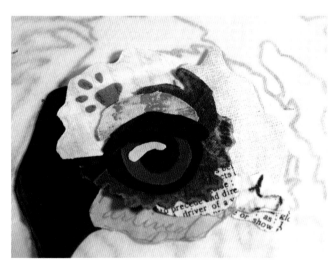

**4.** **Continue to work around the eye, including layers for the eyebrows.** Really study the photo to see the changes in texture and direction of fur around the eyes. This area is great for showcasing a variety of fabric prints.

**5.** **Make the nose.** Remember to keep it simple. Continue to trace and cut fabrics to fill between the eyes and nose.

**6. Work on the ears.** Cut larger areas and fill in with free-cut fur details. Using many thin strips creates the illusion of luscious locks with fine, flyaway hair.

**7. Continue to cut and layer pieces for the body.** If there is a lot of fussy detail in the body fur, cut these shapes more simply. Stitching will add fine details. As you make progress, continue to glue the layers together, making sure they stick to the foundation.

**8. Check all the layers are glued.** Trim away the excess foundation.

**9. Select a background.** With this collage being mostly black and white, it made the options of finding a contrasting background a lot easier. Since the dog's name was Poppy, and I already had this poppy fabric, it was the perfect solution. You might be able to add a personal option like this to your quilt. Glue the collage to the background fabric, layer with batting and a backing fabric. Press.

## Tip

When you feel the collage is complete, take a photo or hang on a design wall. Make sure everything is glued down. Step back from your collage and look at it as a whole. When working, it is very easy to focus on one fabric or area and not see the completed portrait. Decide if you have enough contrast or if any fabrics need replacing. Add or replace fabric pieces now, before stitching.

## Finishing

**10. Quilt as desired.** I made the background simple by outlining the poppies and stitching rows and columns in the blue. This way, the fur and extra detail on the collage stands out more. Don't forget to add the whiskers. Finish the quilt as desired.

# California Quail Jacket

I love to add collage to clothing. It's unexpected and a great way to share what you love, even out in public! Many of the jean jackets I use were purchased either on sale, at a consignment store, or at a thrift shop. A variety of jacket styles will work, or you could even use denim or canvas shirts. Without a huge investment on the project, you can have more fun decorating it. For my jacket project, I chose birds as my initial theme, finally settling on the California quail and some California poppies. Remember you can use any collaged pattern or theme to decorate clothing. Similarly, you can decorate your jacket like mine or make your own creation. Enjoy your happy, decorated collage jacket and see if anyone notices!

## SUPPLIES
- Quail pattern (page 149)
- Poppy pattern (page 145)
- Upcycled jean jacket or shirt
- Vellum or parchment paper
- Collage supplies (page 13)
- Sewing machine and supplies (page 13)

## FABRICS
- Thirteen 6" x 9" (15.2 x 22.9cm) fabric pieces: assorted colors (browns, golds, reds, gray, black, and white) in small prints or solids to match birds
- Scraps or small pieces of various green and orange fabrics in light, medium, and dark values for poppies
- 3" x 18" (7.6 x 45.7cm) green fabric strip for the grass or ground
- Light green fabric for grass sprigs

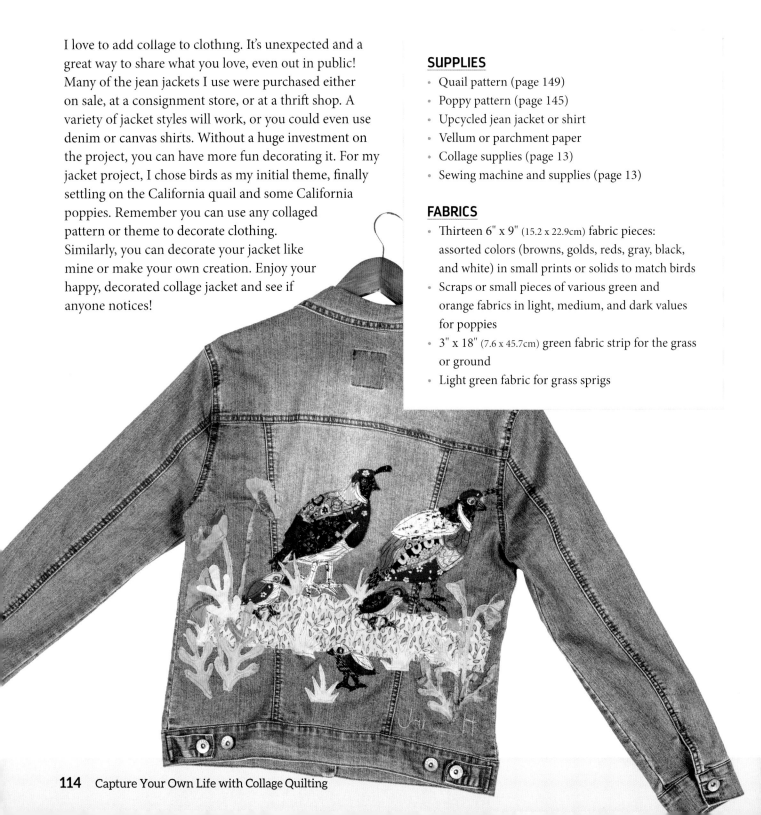

# Making the Collage

**1. Layer the parchment paper over the pattern.** This will prevent the glue and fabrics from sticking to your pattern. We are not using a foundation here. Attach with a little tape. It can be helpful to lay out your fabrics next to your reference photos to make sure you have the full palette you desire.

**2. Make one collaged quail.** I started with the wing because I wanted the body to stand out with bold colors. For inspiration, look at photos of quail in the wild to see the colors and patterns in their feathers.

**3. Once you are happy with your placement, glue the pieces.** Since there is no foundation, you are only gluing pieces to one another. Make sure you leave space around the edges to add more fabric underneath.

**4. Construct two more adult and four baby quails.** The birds can be identical or use a variety of fabrics. I used the same fabrics but mixed up where they went to give an overall cohesion while making the quails look unique. Two adults and three babies will go on the back, while one adult and baby will go on the front. Choose which ones will be paired together.

**5. Construct nine poppies.** Use the poppies and leaves from the wildflower pattern to make a variety of colorful flowers. Do not be afraid of free-cutting your shapes—the pattern is only a guide. Your piece will look more interesting with a little variety.

**6. Lay the green fabric strip at the base for the ground.** Trim so the top edge is wavy, a more natural look. Free-cut seven grass sprigs. Or sketch on the light green fabric with a chalk marker, creating small patches with flat bases and 4–5 spikes at the top.

**7. Arrange the jacket back on your worktable so it is flat.** In the center, lay down the grass strip, add the quail, sprigs, poppies, and leaves. Overlap some of the elements for a more natural look. Pin in place. Try the jacket on; if possible, preview in a mirror or take a photo. When you are happy with your layout, glue the collage pieces in place. Remove the pins as you go.

## Tip

Avoid gluing the pieces where leaves or poppies overlay the quail. Just leave the pins in place and stitch the quail when it comes to quilting. This helps with the flow of the stitching, so you are not having to stop and start many times. After this is complete, you can glue down the leaves and poppies, then stitch.

# Stitching and Finishing

**8. Choose a bobbin thread color that will blend into the inside color of the jacket.** Use black thread to stitch the quail, green for the leaves, and orange for the poppies. Make sure your jacket isn't folded so the stitch only goes through the back.

**9. Arrange more collage elements on the front of the jacket.** You can choose to decorate the shoulder areas. My collage was added to the lower sections near the pockets. I did run into the issue of not being able to machine stitch the collage where it covered the pockets: if I stitched through all the layers, the pockets would no longer function! To remedy this, I used a simple running stitch to hand stitch these collage pieces in place.

# Travel Journal Quilt

**FINISHED SIZE: 36" X 36"** (91.4 X 91.4CM)

I recently visited the UK and fell in love with the Cotswolds. This historic region is located between London and Birmingham in the south of England. I was drawn to the simple beauty of the villages, the variety of cottages, and the charm of their construction in Cotswold stone. I brought home postcards, maps, and photos, then delved into researching the history of that region.

I decided I would put together a composition-style quilt that combines the visual elements that I loved. These included a map and my memories from that visit. I chose to surround these elements with an array of honey, gold, and tan fabrics that complement the stone color of the cottages. The collaged element that I added were two hollyhock stalks, which relate to a photo I took of flowers in front of a row of cottages in Chipping Campden. Including a larger, colorful unit brings cohesion to the quilt. It is placed in such a way that it covers some of the vertical piecing, laying over some of the other parts to visually soften the quilt.

The instructions given are how I made my Cotswold quilt. Composition quilts are made in an improv style, so use my directions as a guide. To make your own version of this quilt, gather photos, saved ephemera, tourist brochures, or maps from a vacation. Start by printing pieces onto fabric sheets, paint a map, make a collage, and arrange on a design wall to form a cohesive design. Your collage elements could include birds, animals, and food associated with the area or kayaks, bikes, or other vacation memories unique to your trip.

## SUPPLIES

- Hollyhocks collage pattern
- Memorabilia: 3 postcards, 7 photographs, printed map, typed Cotswold history
- Black permanent marker
- Freezer paper
- Liquid fabric stabilizer spray
- Collage supplies (page 13)
- Sewing machine and supplies (page 13)

## FABRIC PAINTING SUPPLIES

- Map for reference
- Fabric or acrylic paints in greens and blues
- Large flat paintbrush
- Water container
- Palette or plate for mixing colors
- Plastic table covering

## FABRICS

- Printable fabric sheets
- Dark red and green fabrics for flowers
- Assorted honey-colored fabric pieces and sashing strips for the borders
- 6½" x 13" (16.5 x 33cm) black fabric for letters
- 18" x 18" (45.7 x 45.7cm) white fabric for the map
- 38" x 38" (96.5 x 96.5cm) cotton batting
- 38" x 38" (96.5 x 96.5cm) backing fabric

# Painting the Map Fabric

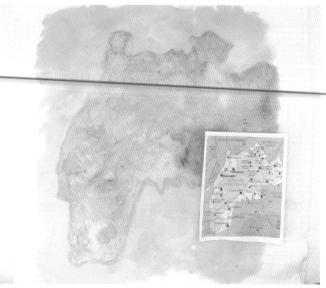

**1. Use a pencil to draw a simple, enlarged map on the white fabric.** I referenced a couple of maps to draw out details like roads, boundaries, towns, and rivers onto the fabric. I keep it as accurate as possible, but it is an artistic interpretation.

**2. Dilute acrylic or fabric paints to make them easier to blend.** Use a large paintbrush to fill in the colors on the map. Allow paint to dry between colors so it does not bleed. Paint in rivers, towns, and other details. Using a black permanent pen, write in the names of towns, counties, rivers, etc.

# Making the Flowers

**3. Make the two flower stalks.** I enlarged a pattern of two hollyhocks and included flowers, leaves, and buds. When making collage flowers, I find it easier to tape parchment paper over the design instead of using a foundation fabric.

**4. Use different values in the fabrics you choose to add interest and depth.** Veins in the leaves should stand out. If leaf clusters blend too much together, try using a different green or add fabric for contrast.

# Assembling the Quilt

**5. Print out your words or dates at your desired size.** Trace these onto the paper side of the freezer paper. These can be drawn freehand. Iron the shiny side of the paper onto your fabric that has been stiffened with stabilizer spray. Cut out the letters along the drawn line.

**6. Print out memorabilia at 5" x 7"** (12.7 x 17.8cm) **and 8" x 10"** (20.3 x 25.4cm) **onto your fabric sheets.** These can include maps, tickets, postcards (printed front and back), brochures, etc. Pin your map unit onto a design wall or similar surface. Arrange other units around the painted map sides. Remember you will add fabric sashing. Pin on the collaged flowers last so they overlay other pieces which will soften some of the straight lines. Step back and look. Remember the design is fluid at this time and can easily change.

# Making the Quilt   All seam allowances are ¼" (6mm).

**7. Cut and add pieced borders around photos.** Use sashing to join the units together. Stitch smaller units together to create larger ones. Attach units around the map. Measure a lot as the borders you cut will need to be cut to size or trimmed to fit together. Press seams. As you work, check your progress on the design wall. Pin on the collage flowers and postcards that will be added later. Include a blank space to add your lettering. Take more photos.

**8. Continue piecing and adding sashing strips.** Finish when the quilt is the correct size and shape. Glue the letters in place on your quilt, then remove freezer paper. Collage flowers and postcards are pinned on.

## Postcards

Photocopy both sides of postcards onto fabric sheets. Trim down, leaving a ¼" (6mm) border. Press the border under on all four sides. These will be topstitched later. Postcards can lay straight or at an angle; I chose to angle mine for variety. Write memories with a permanent pen on the blank side of the postcard, as if you were sending these from your vacation.

# Stitching and Finishing

**9. Stitch-in-the-ditch around the photographs.** Use a walking foot and a monofilament or lightweight thread. Using free-motion stitching and the same lightweight thread, stitch around details in the photographs and stitch horizontal lines in areas of writing. Topstitch the postcards around the outer edge with the lightweight thread. Free-motion quilt if desired.

**10. Change to a colored thread and stitch contour patterns on the map.** Stitch in your sashing with straight lines or a filler stitch. Return to the design wall. Pin the flowers, lettering, and additional postcards in place. Glue.

**11. Free-motion stitch the flowers with a variety of colored and variegated threads.** Stitch around the outer edge of each letter with a matching thread. Once fully quilted over, press and trim to size. Add a binding or finish as desired. Include a personalized label on the back.

# Bed-Size Maxi Quilt

**FINISHED SIZE: 63" X 83"** (160 X 210.8CM)

In this final project, I want to show how you can make a large-scale collage using a pattern enlarged from a photo. Don't be put off by the size of this collage; it just takes a little more time and the pieces are larger. It's wonderful to see collage used as a bed quilt and would be a great addition to any bedroom theme. To make this quilt large enough to fit a bed, I combined the collage and its background with several plain and pieced borders. As this quilt will be used and washed frequently, I tried to keep the collage pieces large, and I stitched around all of them.

The fabrics I used for this project were supplied by Moda Fabrics. These included various colors of Grunge fabric and two "layer cakes" of 10" (25.4cm) squares from the Celestial collection by Zen Chic. My idea for this quilt was for a scrappy look, which I achieved by combining the squares for the background and including a scrappy, pieced border.

I washed this quilt after it was completed as I wanted to see how the collage would fair in the washing machine. Washing encourages bed quilts to be soft, unlike wall quilts, which I generally don't wash. I am happy to report that while there was some fraying, it was not that bad. I enjoy the "loved" look and feel of the quilt.

## SUPPLIES
- Pattern (create your own, page 41)
- 8" x 10" (20.3 x 25.4cm) photo in color
- 30" x 55" (76.2 x 139.7cm) interfacing or stabilizer for foundation
- Collage supplies (page 13)
- Sewing machine and supplies (page 13)
- Quilting ruler
- Rotary cutter and cutting mat

## FABRICS
- 2 layer cakes or eighty 10" (25.4cm) squares
- 10 different fat quarters of coordinating fabrics
- Two 4" x 4" (10.2 x 10.2cm) fabric colors for the eyes
- 6 yards (5.5m) backing fabric
- Eight 2½" (5.5m) x WOF strips for binding
- Cotton batting for a twin-size quilt

# Making the Collage

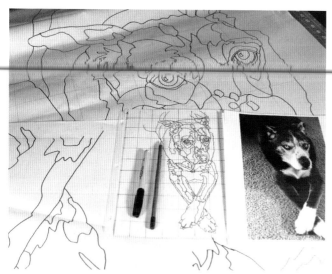

**1. Enlarge pattern from the photo at 500%.** Use the grid-to-grid technique (page 31).

**2. Select your fabrics.** The collage was made using dark fabrics with contrasting lighter, patterned fabrics. When selecting fabrics to use, I let the dog photo guide my value choices. Look through your fabrics and make a rough layout as to where you will use the different colors. Take a photo to help be your guide.

**3. Start with the eyes.** Cut and layer the fabric pieces. Echo the blue iris with another blue to make the color pop. Glue when you are happy.

**4. Continue to work on the face and ears.** This large collage will be part of a bed quilt and therefore washed, so the shapes cut can be larger and less fussy. Only around the eyes did I use small pieces. Remember, all the fabric pieces will be stitched around. While you won't get as much detail in, these prints are capturing details like the spots on the nose. It's important to choose your fabric carefully in these cases.

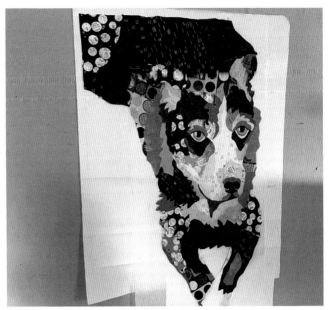

**5. Continue with the body and larger details.** Small details are only found around the feet. With this large collage, I had to fold part of the pattern as I was working and have other areas hanging over the table. It's important to make sure all pieces are glued down. When you are happy with your collage, check the glue then press.

**6. Trim away the excess foundation.** Pin your collage to a design wall and take photos. Check if there any changes you need to make.

## Making the Background

**7. Select a background.** I could have used a single piece of fabric, but I chose to stitch the 10" (25.4cm) squares "on point" (used as diamonds rather than squares). I used my design wall to lay them out before, after, and during the stitching process. When the background was complete, I repositioned the collage on top and glued it into place.

**8. Complete the center panel.** Measure it, making sure it is "square." Trim any excess fabric if necessary. Because this quilt is so large, you may need to take it one section at a time. It's important to use a quilt ruler and accurate measurements to avoid cutting incorrectly.

**9. Add borders.** I added a ¾" (1.9cm) gray inner border, cut at 1¼" (3.2cm). Then a 2" (5.1cm) green border, cut at 2½" (6.4cm). The outer border was made using 9" (22.9cm) squares. I alternated a square-in-square block design with a basic log cabin block. All strips of fabric in the outer border are cut at 3½" (8.9cm).

**10. Continue with borders to reach the desired quilt size.** To make the squares fit the length of the quilt, I added an extra 3" (7.6cm) strip near the bottom on both sides. The final border is a 1½" (3.8cm) gray border, cut at 2" (5.1cm). Press all your seams and make sure the collage is glued to the quilt top.

## Stitching and Finishing    All seam allowances are ¼" (6mm).

**11. Cut the batting and backing fabrics about 6" (15.2cm) larger than the quilt top.** Prepare the backing fabric to the size required and join panels if necessary. Layer your backing, batting, and quilt top in your preferred method. Smooth to remove any wrinkles in the fabrics. Baste. Set your machine up for free-motion quilting. Choose colored threads for the stitching and a bobbin thread color that will blend with the backing fabric. I chose about six different threads, with three being variegated colors.

**12. Quilt the collage.** Remember to stitch around every piece approximately $\frac{1}{16}$" (1.6mm) from the edge of the fabric. Change thread color as desired.

**13. Stitch the background of the collage.** Your aim is to use an even amount of stitching across the whole quilt. Do not quilt as densely on this bed quilt as you would for a wall hanging or it will become too stiff. Stitch the borders, working out from the center of the quilt. Have fun with the details, such as stitching your name and the name of the quilt.

**14. Trim the quilt to remove excess batting and backing fabric.** Add binding. Wash and dry your quilt on a gentle cycle for a soft finish.

# chapter 4

# Gallery

## Work by Author

I started making fabric collage quilts in 2003. I am self-taught but was initially inspired by Susan Carlson on an episode of *Simply Quilts* with Alex Anderson. Seeing Susan using raw-edge fabrics and glue gave me permission to do the same and opened the doors to my collage style. Susan's work continues to inspire me. My first large quilt, *Pacific Coral Reef*, was entered into a local county fair and won me first place, the Best Novice Quilter award, and a sewing machine! I didn't hold back. I submitted to Paducah in 2004 and the International Quilt Festival in 2005, and my quilts were accepted into both shows. I continue to enter quilts into shows in the USA and around the world. Here are some of my signature quilts made over the last twenty years.

### Jesus Christ, a Lizard!

2011

Quilt size: 26" x 45" (66 x 114.3cm)

After a family vacation to Costa Rica in 2010, I wanted to take some of my wildlife photos and make them into quilts. We witnessed this common basilisk (also called Jesus Christ lizard) walking on water! I used my own hand-dyed fabrics, a painted background, and onion bags to create the water reflection. This quilt was featured in *Quilting Arts* magazine in 2012 and was my first published article.

## Pacific Coral Reef

2004

Quilt size: 44" x 64" (111.8 x 162.6cm)

My very first collage quilts were fish quilts like the ones that I had seen Susan Carlson making. When I wanted to make something larger to enter in a show, this was the quilt I designed. It was inspired by the USPS stamp set called "Pacific Coral Reef" that was available in 2004.

## Nameless Afghan Girl

2013

Quilt size: 24" x 24" (61 x 61cm)

For many years I saved this famous cover image from *National Geographic* magazine, thinking it would be wonderful to make in collage. After seeing a call for an exhibition called "Notable Woman," I gathered fabric I had painted and hand dyed, drew out my design, and constructed this quilt. After receiving permission from the photographer Steve McCurry, I entered my quilt into the show. It was accepted and used on the cover of the exhibition catalogue. This quilt was noticed by Shanker and Mala Ramakrishna in Dubai, and I was invited to teach a Faces Fabric Collage Workshop at the Dubai International Quilt Show in 2020.

## Our Maine Event

2016

Quilt size: 32" x 33" (81.3 x 83.8cm)

On vacation I love to journal, take photos, and save all the maps, tickets, etc. Preserving these memories by combining them into a quilt seems like the perfect project. This quilt represents our family vacation to Acadia National Park in Maine, USA. It was a fun adventure with many memorable activities. This technique was featured on *Quilting Arts TV* and in *Quilting Arts* magazine in September 2017.

## Cosmo

2017

Quilt size: 18" x 18" (45.7 x 45.7cm)

This small quilt was the first time I tried using an abstract, bright color palette for an animal quilt. I followed no rules when choosing my colors and fabrics. This can make the process harder than simply copying what you see. Using the black background was an easy solution and contrasts well with the brightly colored bulldog.

## Bullseye x Nine

2018

Quilt size: 59" x 58" (149.9 x 147.3cm)

I couldn't resist taking a photo of this dog named Bullseye, who was white with a black patch over his eye. For my pattern, I simplified the design, making pattern pieces using freezer paper. I was able to iron them onto my fabrics and cut them out. I used this technique because I knew I wanted to repeat the dog collage a number of times. *Bullseye x Nine* won Best of Show at my local quilt show and first place at the California State Fair.

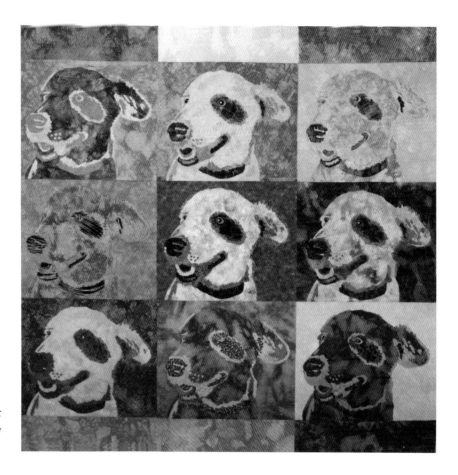

## City Slickers

2019

Quilt size: 30" x 28" (76.2 x 71.1cm)

After visiting England and seeing artwork that featured cows, I decided this would be the next theme for my quilts. The name for the quilt was inspired by the background fabric and the ranching movie of the same name. Using scraps in bright colors, combined with blacks and darker value fabrics, was a new adventure for me. Owned by a private collector.

## Gentle Giant

2019

Quilt size: 30" x 50" (76.2 x 127cm)

I made this quilt for an exhibit called "A Better World." I did a lot of research into the conservation of giraffes and found out that their numbers in the wild are fewer than we imagine. I like to support the work of the Giraffe Conservation Foundation, and when I sold my other giraffe quilt called *Melman, the Vulnerable Giraffe*, I donated half my proceeds to this cause. For the background of this quilt, I layered various fabrics from vintage silks, denim, and upholstery fabrics.

## Big Frank

2020

Quilt size: 48" x 68" (121.9 x 172.7cm)

I made *Big Frank* in 2020, a few months into the pandemic. I was stuck at home and had the time to work on a large project. The enlargement was 700% and is the largest pet portrait I have made so far. When gathering my fabrics, I chose to use old and ugly ones, which happen to work perfectly in this quilt. *Big Frank* received the Best Use of Color award at the Mid-Atlantic Quilt Festival in 2022 and a Judges Choice award at Festival of Quilts 2022.

## Three Ladies

2021

Quilt size: 39" x 19" (99.1 x 48.3cm)

I teach a rooster workshop and have several different chicken patterns. Here, I wanted to explore making more hen patterns as they have such great character. The chicken photos I used were from my sister-in-law, whose chickens have great names like Myrtle, Ivy, Olive, and Petunia. For the background, I used velvet, silk, and hand-dyed pieces, layered with a green chiffon scarf.

## Max

2021

Quilt size: 28" x 38" (71.1 x 96.5cm)

I made this pet portrait quilt as a commission. I love the perspective of how the dog is lying down with the paws in the foreground. I used the same pattern enlarged at 500% to make *Maxi*, the bed-sized quilt project on page 124.

## Wildflowers and War

2022

Quilt size: 32" x 32" (81.3 x 81.3cm)

Lupines that grow in my backyard have
become an obsession for me. I painted them
using watercolors and then made them using
fabric scraps. In the Wildflower Runner
project (page 84), you will see the same
lupines included in the pattern. I wanted to
make a larger quilt and combine a collaged
animal with the flowers. I made many flower
stems first, constructed the rabbit, then
combined for the composition. This quilt sold
in Fall 2022 at the International Quilt Festival
in Houston and is owned by a private collector.

## Loch Leven Lakes

2022

Quilt size: 36" x 36" (91.4 x 91.4cm)

This final quilt was completed using samples that
I made in the process of writing this book. My
hiking boots seemed like good subject matter for
the collage demonstrations, the background was
part of the Simple Layered Landscapes project
(page 66), and the stitching is included in the
free-motion quilting section. My inspirational
photo for this quilt was taken from my tent while
on a backpacking weekend at Loch Leven Lakes
in the Sierra Nevada Mountains, California.

# Work by Students

I am thrilled when students share their finished work with me. As a teacher, I see a completed project as a sign that the student enjoyed the process, invested their time in finishing, and is proud and excited to share that work. For me, that is the icing on the cake. Thank you to the students who offered up their completed quilts to be included in this book. I really appreciate it. I hope you enjoy looking at these unique quilts and see how people interpret my instructions and patterns in their own unique ways.

PHOTO CREDIT: TERRIE PEETS

## Mango, our Blue Weimaraner

**by Terrie Peets**

Quilt size: 14" x 14" (35.6 x 35.6cm)

"This was my very first collage appliqué quilt taught to me by Jane Haworth. It was so much fun, giving me freedom for my creativity. This is Mango, our blue Weimaraner, who is four years old and hails from Montana. He is the one who gets us out of bed in the morning and makes us get more exercise by walking him in the Sierra Nevada backyard."

## Shadow

**by Keila Classen**

Quilt size: 23" x 28" (58.4 x 71.1cm)

"As a perfectionist and someone who doesn't view themselves as an artist, I was hesitant to take this class because I didn't think creating a pet portrait was within my reach as a quilter. I ended up signing up last minute on a whim just to get some exposure to collage quilting for other purposes. I was frankly shocked at how successfully I was able to represent my dog Shadow's appearance and personality following Jane's method and instructions. As a teacher myself, I recognize how good instruction can offset student lack of confidence. I'm so grateful my willingness to risk failure was met with Jane's clear instructions and thoughtful feedback, allowing me to create something I'm deeply proud of. Shadow is slipping into his senior years, and making this wall hanging was also a way for me to embody my love for him into something tangible: a reminder to cherish the time I still have with him."

## Ted

**by Cecile Brown**

Quilt size: 18" x 24" (45.7 x 61cm)

"I really enjoyed the process and am enjoying the finished portrait of my dog, Ted. I liked the process so much that I made two more pieces—one of my daughter's cat."

## Juno

**by Audrey Vallen**

Quilt size: 21" x 29½" (53.3 x 74.9cm)

"I really enjoyed Jane's collage process. Starting with the enlarged outline of my pet, which broke the image down into a map of lights and darks, I was then able to free-cut bits of fabric to fill the shapes and build the image. Jane provided great guidance on the critical areas of eyes and nose, so the result would look lifelike. It was great fun diving into my fabric scraps and sometimes finding unlikely, but fabulous, choices to make this collage of our beloved dog!"

## Yoshi

**by Suzanne Timmer**

Quilt size: 20" x 27" (50.8 x 68.6cm)

"It is a portrait of my dog, Yoshi. Yoshi passed away 2 months prior to the quilt show. I was very sad and depressed after Yoshi died. The process of making the quilt provided me with a way to honor my loyal companion of 11 years and helped me to allow myself to grieve. I enjoy making art quilts. This was a new technique for me. I love 'painting' with fabric."

## Curiosity

**by Georgia Williams**

Quilt size: 24" x 24" (61 x 61cm)

"I was so lucky to take a COVID-lockdown Zoom class from Jane. I loved Jane, the process, and the Zoom format, although in person would have even been better. Jane explained things so well and gave great feedback. I love her process as so many teachers feel the project has to be done just so, but Jane's process was more spontaneous. If the piece didn't fit or the color was just not right, it was not a problem with her method. It could be fixed easily and made the whole process so much more enjoyable and attainable."

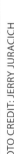

## Posy: A Cow Full of Flowers

**by Sandy Juracich**

"Cows have been my favorite animal (besides cats) since I was a child. When I saw that Jane was giving a workshop on 'Colorful Cows' virtually in October 2020, I immediately signed up. This was a transformative class for me. Making art quilts is what I truly enjoy. I used many fabrics from the Kaffe Fassett Collective because I love the vibrant colors and large floral patterns. I finished the quilt in February 2021 in San Jose, CA."

## Orson

**by Donna Eck**

Pillow size: 18" x 18" (45.7 x 45.7cm)

"I can't recall how I came across Jane's Pet Portraits class, but I do remember being instantly captivated by the whimsical, colorful dog portraits created from tiny bits of fabric. I immediately signed up for Jane's class. Not having a dog of my own, I chose Orson, a scruffy Brussels Griffon owned by singer/songwriter LP to be my subject. I figured I would make the quilt and give it to her as a gift. Like assembling a jigsaw puzzle, with each placement of a piece of fabric, a face starts to appear. It's amazing how easy it is to capture the personality of a beloved pet with fabric collage. I ultimately turned my quilt into a pillow and gave it to LP at the next concert of hers that I attended."

## The Lizard Quilt

### by Becky MacKellar

Quilt size: 20" x 24" (50.8 x 61cm)

"I took Jane's lizard quilt class in Houston in the fall of 2019. I found this a hard technique for me to do. I had never done anything like it. I mostly just sat in the class not doing anything. I finally conquered it in February 2021. I admit to using fusible web instead of glue. I have also finished two collaged portraits as well. Jane was an excellent teacher."

## Red Sunflower

### by Lydia Stevenson

Quilt size: 20" x 20" (50.8 x 50.8cm)

"I took your class online during late 2020. The background is filled with sequins. I absolutely loved your class and the great results from my first collage quilt."

PHOTO CREDIT: BARBRA CLARK

## Pillows

### by Barbra Clark

"*A Rose for Rose* was made for my daughter-in-law, *Suzy's Kitty* was a gift for my sister, and *Wild Horse* was a donation to a charity auction for military service members. I enjoyed the process, and it was much easier than I thought it would be! It was fun auditioning different fabrics to achieve different effects and color combinations. The finished product is amazing!"

## Three Portraits

**by Marta James**

"I took Jane's online class as soon as it was available, at the beginning of the pandemic. Since then, I have done many pet portraits for family and friends (no sales involved). It has actually kept me busy when I needed to be. I enjoyed it."

## Rudy

**by Lori Learned**

Quilt size: 24" x 24" (61 x 61cm)

"It was perfect starting with the eyes and working out from there. It really allowed me to show his personality. My class with Jane took a complicated process and broke it into manageable, and fun, parts. I love the finished picture."

## Murphy

**by Lynne Dees**

Quilt size: 24" x 22" (61 x 55.9cm)

"Having been a student in two of Jane's pet portrait classes, I am amazed at the different approaches taken by fellow students toward their pieces—some are extremely detailed and realistic, while others are more abstract and whimsical. Using a large, high-resolution photograph as a starting point is a key factor in creating a successful portrait. However, students always seem to successfully eke out the character of their pet from even a less-than-stellar image."

# chapter 5

# Patterns

## Hummingbirds

Photocopy at 125%

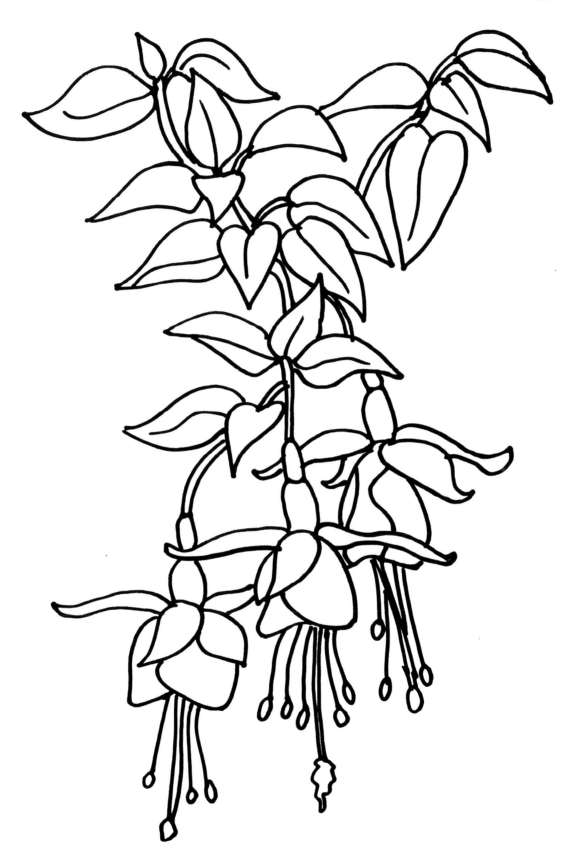

# Cat

Photocopy at 125%

# Guitar

Photocopy at 125%

# Seashells

Photocopy at 125%

# Index

# About the Author

PHOTO CREDIT: BONNIE MCCAFFERY

Born in Devon, England, Jane grew up with a love for arts, crafts, and textiles. She received a degree in Textile Design with a focus on weaving and went on to work in a Laura Ashley clothing factory. Moving to California with her young family in 1998, Jane became aware of traditional quilting and quickly became hooked. With a desire to design her own art quilts, she educated herself with all things quilting and art quilting. As her hobby slowly grew into a full-time career, she taught sewing arts locally to both children and adults. Jane now teaches nationally and internationally to quilt guilds, quilt shops, and quilt shows.

She now lives in northern California with her family who love to explore California, camp, and visit family in England.

**Follow me on social media:**
Website: janehaworth.com (sign up for a newsletter and patterns available in my shop)
Facebook: jane.z.haworth and Fabric Collage School
Instagram: janehquilter, #creativecollagequilts, and #creativecollagequilting
Pinterest: janehh22